HushAndDo

An inward journey of self-examination
to transition from mere talk to action

Jay T. Hairston II

Published by The Hairston Company LLC

Printed in the United States of America

HushAndDo

ISBN; 978-0-578-42351-7

For permission requests, write to the address below.

Jay T. Hairston II

HushAndDo@gmail.com

***

Edited by Diane Walters

www.dianewalters-writer.com

Book design and layout by Amanda Lott

Lotts of Designs, LLC.

www.lottsofdesigns.com

I would like to dedicate this book

to my future self.

I write this to give you a chance.

Contents

Acknowledgments

I want to thank my God. Your words spoken through me in this book give breath and life first to me and foremost. Your utterances have resuscitated a wounded soul and have given me hope to forge ahead yet again. I truly love You and thank You.

Christine, thank you for believing in me. I know who I am and where I'm headed in life. It all may not have fully appeared yet, but you remain at my side, believing with me and believing in me. Thank you for being my patient support even when I have doubted myself. I love our marriage, our chemistry, our friendship, and our teamwork.

To my children—Brooklyn, my darling firstborn, thank you for being so patient with Daddy as I finished this book. It's finally finished. Now we can play.

To Bailey, our newest addition to the Hairston home, I love you dearly. If you let me sleep, Daddy can start on *HushAndDo,* the children's book, and you can be one of the first to read it!

To my loving and actively involved parents—thank you for encouraging me and being my test subjects. Whether I emailed you rough drafts of chapters or had you thumb through pages of cover designs and edits—you were there with me the entire time.

Good Brotha—thank you for equipping me with a decent lexicon. I endeavor to be a sesquipedalian but hopefully never too esoteric.

Mom—thank you for gifting me with creativity and a willingness to try new things and think outside the boxes of tradition. I know I'm not "none of your lil' friends," but you are my Girl!

To my siblings—thank you all for spreading the word of this movement and for being among the first to purchase shirts and hoodies. You all were quick to represent anything having to do with *HushAndDo.*

I want to especially acknowledge and thank my research assistants: Quaniesha Murphy and Precious Boone. Quaneisha introduced me to key psychologists and their research, all which have influenced and shaped this work. Precious sifted through numerous articles to find the right ones suitable for my points. Both of you have bright futures in social psychology and social work.

When I first uttered the words "hush and do" in the beginning of 2017, it was Johnny Parker who grabbed a hold of it and promoted it on social media. He is one of Cleveland's best hearts. What began as a humorous catchphrase has turned into something more. Thank you!

To every person who believed in this movement and pushed me to take it to the next level – thank you. Whether you bought the *HushAndDo* T-shirt, the hoodie, sported the wristband, or merely cc'd me on social media every time you used the phrase, I sincerely thank you.

Finally, I want to honor the legacy of preaching and my late grandfather, Bishop M.D. Borden Jr. There are no words to describe how much I miss him. As my ministry begins to incorporate more preaching and teaching, I believe he'd be proud to know that his eldest grandson is still doing the work of the Lord.

I'll see you in the morning,

Little Papa

Introduction

I cannot deny or downplay who I am. I am a Christian minister and an adherent to the Judeo-Christian faith. My faith and spirituality lay at the core of who I am, and they inform and shape my identity. I realize others may not have the same faith passion that I do. Some may pick up this book who don't even adhere to any particular faith or deity. I welcome all audiences, be it henotheistic, monotheistic, polytheistic, atheistic, agnostic, gnostic, pantheistic, animistic, etc. Because of who I am, I will employ several religious sources to explicate the statutes of this work. I will chiefly use the Bible, but not exhaustively.

The entire piece will weave between personal opinion, as the result of careful research and experience, scholarly psychological study, and ancient religious texts, undertaking a balanced approach to the principles of *HushAndDo*. Some sections will lean more toward faith and spiritual devotion; whereas, others will read more informatively and pedagogically. This is not an attempt to jam religion or any particular theology down your throat, but only to elucidate points. Regardless of your position on faith and theology, I believe the precepts in this book will be beneficial to your journey of becoming. Perhaps you may read something that will challenge your current beliefs or badger long-standing worldviews. I welcome that as well. I love God and have committed my soul, heart, life, and time to loving and serving Him and His people, for which I offer no apology. However, you do not have to nor am I pressuring you to do the same in this book. Nonetheless, if you happen to encounter His love while you read, which I sincerely hope you do, then feel free to contact me. This is a book for all. I invite you to have an open heart and an open mind.

HushAndDo isn't just about the clever hashtag (#HushAndDo) or motivational speaking alone. There are plenty of people in the world who do that already. They are accomplishing goals at accelerated rates in excellence, and I applaud their successes, but I'm not here for that.

To call *HushAndDo* a motivational endeavor alone and to refer to me as a motivational speaker, though the book contains some of those elements, is limiting. We are motivated to do many things, and people accomplish various goals worldwide.

However, what happens when we lose motivation? If motivation was our source of strength to move ahead in life and pursue dreams, callings, and goals, then how could we ever do any of that in its absence? Indeed, we lose motivation sometimes. What do we lean on when it's lost? I'm not damning motivational speakers or criticizing the good work they do. There are undoubtedly some motivational aspects of *HushAndDo*; however, it is not our primary undertaking, and it's not our movement's essential goal. *HushAndDo* is about Transformational Thinking and Transformational Living—the journey toward doing what we seek to do and becoming what we're to become—together, through its ups and downs, being perfectly imperfect human beings throughout the process. I want to be changed and transformed in the way I think and live. Ultimately, I want others to experience that same transformation. I embrace my humanness completely, consisting of mind, body, heart/soul, and spirit. We were not created to be non-thinking and non-feeling robots, mechanically programmed to list goals, accomplish them, and then create new ones. I want to experience the journey of this life and take deliberate time to traverse the path of self-discovery. I challenge us to look deeply within ourselves and consider where we can transform our thinking, which will lead to transforming our living. The message of *HushAndDo* is a self-reflective path toward personal revolution.

I echo the words of Richard J. Foster in saying, "We must always remember that the path does not produce the change; it only places us where the change can occur."[a]

Not only is it about changing the way we think, but it also addresses wholeness. I believe we need to investigate certain issues of the self, and through this introspection, we can arrive at a better knowledge of self. The Honorable Elijah Muhammad said in *Message to the Black-Man*, "First, my people must be taught the knowledge of self. Then and only then will they be able to understand others and that which surrounds them."[b] Although this was written to Black people

---

[a] Richard J. Foster, *Celebration of Discipline, The Path to Spiritual Growth* (New York: Harper, San Francisco, 1998).

[b] Elijah Muhammad, *Message to the Blackman* (Arizona: Secretarius MEMPS Publications), 39

suffering under the Jim Crow law and injustice during the Civil Rights Movement, the message applies universally to all. As we begin to understand ourselves better, how we process, how we recharge our energy, how we communicate, our orientation to change, the ways we make decisions, our weaknesses and fears, as well as our strengths and passions, we can better formulate strategies to achieve the things we want in life and to become the people we desire to be. You must know who you are and be open to wrestling with the good and the not-so-good parts of who you are. Denial will ultimately lead to denial. If we fail to come to grips with the various components of who we are, then this will lead to the things we want in life being denied to us.

I realized not long ago that I had quite the affection for attention, and still do in some ways. Therefore, I always announced my moves to gain attention. I realized that I wanted attention and affirmation and praise more than I wanted the actual completion of my goals and dreams. Announcing that I was going to write a book, record a CD, or start a business garnered me the praise and admiration of having written a book, recorded a CD, and started a business but *without* having actually done any of it. I was cheating myself, reaping the benefits of having accomplished something but not doing it. Cheating—I will reveal the depths of this in more detail in complete transparency later. It's pertinent to mention it now because this is the level of transparency in which you must walk to start transforming your thinking and transforming your life.

HushAndDo seeks to bridge the gap between young millennials, Generation Z'ers to Generation X'ers, and baby boomers too. We millennials are inundated with information due to the proliferation of the World Wide Web. We are intimately connected to our smartphones, tablets, and iPads, and devoted to technology. With the advent of social media and the Internet, we are a generation of innovation and mass communication. Sometimes, older generations aren't able to understand the millennials and Generation X'ers. I believe we senior millennials stand in the gap between these generations because we are old enough to remember life before the advancements of modern technology, yet we are at the forefront of many breakthroughs in tech as we know it today. We had to take handwritten notes in class in a physical notebook. We remember the time where it wasn't assumed that every home had a computer. We had to find a pay phone or use someone's house phone to contact family and friends when away from home. We didn't have cyberspace constantly at our fingertips. Speaking of Internet access, we remember not having a wireless field and having to make sure nobody was using the landline, so we could dial-up an Internet connection. We went to physical libraries and looked up books in the card catalog to do research for a paper. A text message back then was writing a handwritten note, folding it in creative ways, and passing it along to friends.

Do you think I'm cute? Check yes or no— crossing our fingers that the "yes" box was checked every time! We had to make sure to rewind the VHS tapes we rented from Blockbuster or Hollywood Video stores before returning them. Those fees were so petty in my opinion, but I was fortunate ***enough*** to never have to pay them! We remember that life well and we lived it. However, we now also remember and currently have lived a life accessible to thousands of technological inventions. We proudly stand in the gap between the past and present. In this information age, we constantly share and receive data rapidly on a daily basis. Sometimes the information can be overwhelming. It can be too much stimulation, and our senses get overwhelmed. Then, we aren't sure what to do or what decisions to make because there are so many options and so many voices, all vying with one another to establish prominence. To remedy that, *HushAndDo* is the still small voice that silences the extenuating voices, amplifies your inner voice, and gently leads you by the hand into your new tomorrows. Hopefully, you now see that this is more than motivation. I highly recommend that you read this book in chronological order as well, as each chapter builds from the previous chapters. This is a journey and one we will take together—a journey of first steps, launching out into new thinking, new behaviors, and enjoying an extended lifelong stay. I would love to hear your testimonies while on this journey. Please feel free to share them with me. I would love to hear from you. Please share and follow me on: Facebook, www.facebook.com/jay.t.hairston; as well as Instagram and Twitter @JayTHairston2.

You may now believe you have a keen sense of what you're getting into by reading this. I give you permission to keep reading to discover just how deep we will descend.

Chapter One

The Hush

Please help yourself to some astounding statistics (2018) about Facebook, Instagram, and Twitter, which you ***may*** or ***may not*** have realized concerning the social-media world. They set the platform for the necessity of our labor.[1]

FACEBOOK

- Facebook has more than 2.27 billion global monthly active users. This is roughly 22 % of the world's population.
- There are 1.47 billion daily active users

- There are roughly 207.36 million Facebook users in the United States
- The average Facebook user has 155 Facebook friends[2]
- Users access Facebook an average of 8 times per day
- More than 50 million small businesses have active Facebook Pages
- The average time spent on Facebook per visit is 20 minutes, making the average monthly time spent 600 minutes
- One in five Facebook videos is now a live broadcast
- Each day, 35 million people update their statuses on Facebook
- The main reason for using Facebook according to worldwide users (as of 2015) was to stay in touch with what family and friends are doing (59 percent). Forty-seven percent use it to stay up to date with news and current events. Forty-six percent use it to fill up spare time. Forty-four percent access Facebook for general networking

with other people. Thirty-eight percent access Facebook to share their opinions.

INSTAGRAM

- As of June 2018, there are roughly 1 billion monthly active Instagram users and 400 million daily active users
- There are 95 million photos uploaded to Instagram every day

TWITTER

- Twitter has 335 million worldwide monthly active users (as of second quarter 2018) and 100 million people who use it on an active daily basis[3]
- 500 million tweets are sent every day.

1.1 May They Have Your Attention Please

- To divert and amuse; to show hospitality to; to admit into or hold in the mind. This is the definition of the verb *entertain.*
- The act or faculty of concentrating the mind on a single object, thought, or event; observant care or consideration. This is how *attention* is defined.[c]
- Lastly, the etymology of the compound verb *entertain* is "to keep up, maintain, to keep (someone) in a certain frame of mind," which comes from an Old French verb *entretenir.* In its Latin roots and most basic form of *entre-tenir*, entre means *among,* and *tenir* means to hold.[d]

---

[c] "entertain," "attention." *Random House Webster's Dictionary*.BallentineBooks, 2001.

[d] "Entertain." *Online Etymology Dictionary*. Douglas Harper, 2019. https://www.etymonline.com/

I absolutely love languages and studying them. Observing their similarities and their differences has helped, in part, to advance my career. I am sharing this because I want to treat a highly complex reality with the most basic care. There are millions upon millions of posts every day on social media. I've only provided some key statistics from Facebook, Twitter, and Instagram. We haven't even begun to consider the entire gamut of popular social-media outlets that exist today: WhatsApp, Viber, Snapchat, Pinterest, LinkedIn, YouTube, and Tumblr. The numbers are exceedingly overwhelming, are they not? Social media, though it connects families and friends across the globe, can also greatly distract us. It sweet-talks us into a place of social comparison and preoccupation with the affairs of others. I'll speak more about the Social Comparison Theory downstream; so stay tuned. The myriad expressions of social media are very hospitable with providing a brief recess from our everyday routines. We connect with others' plights and stories, which is humanity at its finest. These connections occupy space in our mind and hold our attention. We observe the many concepts presented by our social media "friends," daily. Thus, our attentions are captured. We are entertained. They have us, our focus, our energy, and, ultimately, our time.

Consider how easy it is to be distracted by a funny video shared on Facebook that has you and your co-workers laughing throughout the entire day. Think about that one friend you have, who we all have, who seems to have a penchant for controversy and cannot wait to sound off on Facebook about current events. That's usually the same friend who'll spend twenty minutes arguing with you, then suddenly stop to say, "I don't have time to argue with you!" They have even created a meme for such posts that usually has a picture of someone eating popcorn with the caption, "I'm just here for the comments!" Watching the comments and the various responses pour in is quite entertaining. Let's be honest; we love the drama. It pulls us in! Then, what about all the political propaganda populating our feeds? And, it doesn't end there.

Fifty-million businesses have active Facebook accounts. We see countless numbers of advertisements flood our timelines each day. Everybody is trying to get into our minds, our time, and even our pockets.

1.2 How These Stats Hit Home

Now, let's focus on some of these statistics in a manner that directly impacts you and me and *HushAndDo*. If there are roughly 1.94 billion people using Facebook on a monthly basis, then roughly, 737 million people are using Facebook to share their opinion with friends, family, somebody—anybody who will listen—perhaps even you! They seek in some way to entertain you indirectly! I'm not trying to suggest that almost a billion people arise each day to discover ways to capture the audience of you. That would promote a certain air of narcissism to which I don't subscribe and don't recommend. Seven hundred and thirty-seven million people believe they have something to say and don't mind sharing it. Are you overwhelmed yet by the astounding number of social-media voices vying to capture your attention?

I believe it's most appropriate now to unveil one of my areas of struggle and how it birthed *HushAndDo*. I thoroughly take my time to make decisions. I research facts, reviews, and always consult the experts in whichever arena the decision falls. Not only that, but I also consult those with experience. I want to talk to people who have faced the same decisions I am facing; people who have been in my shoes before. I can easily interview hundreds of people and thumb through hundreds of sources before moving forward because I want to make a solid, well-informed, and rational decision with no reluctance or regrets while I forge ahead. Not to boast of my own plumage, but as a result, my strenuous decision-making process has yet to produce a decision I've regretted! This method in my madness of governing my decisions has tested the limits of my wife's patience. She is more of a hands-on and trial-and-error learner to make her decisions. Mine is a sound system, but it has its paralyzing pitfalls: time and procrastination. It takes me quite a long time to make up my mind and to follow through with a decision.

I frequently get mired in the quicksand of information gathering—an information and options overload. The birth of an idea is always vivifying and invigorating, full of momentum, running on a large motor of optimism at high velocity. However, the longer it takes to move forward toward fruition, the more that motor loses its strength—before long, all the momentum is lost, and I find myself trapped in the sunken place of information paralysis. Simply put, there are too many options and too much information to sort through. I'm so bombarded with information, reviews, and opinions that it all becomes increasingly overwhelming. It becomes a heavy weight upon me, like an elephant sitting on my chest. It stifles the breath of whatever I was doing and snatches the life from it. I'm left cemented in the information-gathering stage, never to move forward on any decision. The decision may be the size of a molehill, but the vast mountain of data I've amassed casts an ominous shadow of fear over the entire situation. Fear of making the wrong decision. Fear of misapplying data. Fear that it won't work out for me the way it did for others. Fear of failing. Fear of succeeding, believe it or not. The "what if" questions shorten my breath and stir anxiety. I begin to stress and lose sleep over the decisions. My mind races uncontrollably, seemingly at the speed of light with no slowdown in sight. My chest gets tight as if I had chronic obstructive pulmonary disease.

The rising stress levels affect me emotionally and physically. That which once was a moment of excitement and energy has now become a heavy cross and a lonesome burden to carry: thinking through various scenarios, the way my decision could play out, who it would affect and impact, and researching the depths of my soul to decide if there is a better way to do it—I'm left frozen and unable to move. The collection of advice, Google searches, database searches, social media, reviews, and news opinions has become a torrential deluge that has inundated and entombed me. I am drowned as the last ounce of air is pressed from my lungs. There is no more breath. It has taken me days, weeks, and even months, at times, to arrive at this desperate place of despair, but I'm rescued immediately in a bright flash and saved by saying, "I'll think about this later." I now put the decision on the back burner, so I can get some mental relief. This is one form procrastination takes.

Ironically, we'll deal with procrastination later on! "This" with all the information and intelligence I've gathered remains in the back of my mind, marinating in all its pros and cons, but for now, there will be no decision because it was simply all too overwhelming. But a small voice interrupted me and liberated me from this miry-clay quagmire.

"Hush."

"But I need to be sure this is ri—"

"Hush."

"But what if I'm wro—?"

"Hush."

"Will it work ou—?"

"Hush."

"I don't want to be disappoi—"

"Hush."

"But—"

"Hush. . . . I give you permission to move forward."

1.3 Permission

Everyone has an opinion and something to say. They flood our computers, our phones, and our TV's daily. Gigabytes upon gigabytes of information are available at our fingertips daily, at a moment's notice.

There are almost four-million Google-searches conducted per minute![4] There simply comes a time where we must silence all the voices in our lives. Social media gives everyone something they wouldn't otherwise have had fifteen years ago: a microphone and an audience! The liberating news is that you don't have to sit in their audiences, and you don't have to listen anymore. You have enough information. You've heard from enough people about it. You've read enough books and articles on it. You've talked about it long enough.

Right now, I simply want to gently turn down the volume on everyone and everything trying to speak into your life. We'll gradually fade its noise to zero decibels. The only voice I want you to hear right now is yours. What do you have to say? What do you want? What are you feeling in your gut? I dare you to trust that gut feeling, and go with it. I understand that there is a lot to consider, but not for one more moment can we be stuck with gathering information, afraid to move forward. It's like the child playing at the pool who's afraid to get into the water because it's so cold. She dips her feet in the water and slowly takes her time to fully immerse herself. Or he takes so much time preparing to get into the pool that he's missing all the fun his friends are having—those who are already in the pool because they splashed in. Give me your hand, and let me guide you into the waters of your goals, dreams, and desires. No, we don't have to cannonball into this pool, but we do have to be more deliberate about getting in. We are getting into this water! It's long since been your time to have fun. I give you permission:

I give you permission to take the first step.

I give you permission to take the next step.

I give you permission to keep stepping.

I give you permission to walk.

I give you permission to jog.

I give you permission to run.

I give you permission to adjust your pace as you begin to explore this new place.

I give you permission to be afraid of the uncertainty awaiting your future.

I give you permission to doubt things.

I give you permission to question things.

I give you permission to express the range of emotions you may be experiencing as we journey together.

I give you permission to feel.

I give you permission to be.

I give you permission to be a work in progress.

I give you permission to be a human being.

Hush and Do

The only thing I do not give you permission to do is to stop.

You may be afraid, but you will no longer be paralyzed by your fear. You may be a work in progress, but, whatever happens, keep progressing and keep working. You cannot return to the place of paralysis. You can gather new information as needed while you keep moving forward. Feel whatever emotions you may feel, but keep forging ahead. In a race, you can run backward, stand still, or run forward. If you run backward, I guarantee you'll lose quickly. If you stand still and remain cautious, though it feels safe, eventually you will lose your place and still end up losing. Everybody else will pass you by. It'll just take longer to experience the loss and failure. The only option to ensure completion of the race is to move forward—feel free to walk, jog, or run. Crawl if you have to. Have friends in the race with you to carry you if you're fatigued. Whatever you do, you must keep moving forward. You must continue onward. You cannot quit, and you will not give up. *I won't let you.* There's too much at stake to stop here.

I give you permission to hush yourself, to hush the many voices competing for space and attention in your mind, to hush all doubtful critics and fearful hesitations. You can start doing that now.

As the many utterances begin to be silenced in our lives, let's explore all we can finally do.

Chapter 2

I Need Attention—No! I Need To Be Whole

I used to be the king of announcing everything I was going to do and wanted to do. Any idea that came to my mind, no matter how big or small, even before taking the first steps toward executing it, I would immediately tell someone. I didn't just tell a few people, but I made grand announcements and illustrious social-media posts to let as many people as possible know what I was going to do. I had ideas to do concept music albums, such as my first recording: "The Disappearing Act." There are so many things for which I've found an affinity, and regardless of what it was, I always prioritized announcing it. I told everybody my moves all the time, always declaring my intentions. I realized I was a real-life manifestation of the parable of the sower (Matthew 13:1–9). I was nothing more than a rapid-sprouting seed planted in rocky ground and shallow soil. As my ideas sprang up, just as hurriedly I would spring up announcements about those ideas, but unfortunately, they had shallow roots. I believe they were amazing ideas, yet as quickly as they emerged, they quickly perished. For example, I would tell people about books I considered writing. Before even a single stroke of my pen touched the paper, I had already told hundreds of people about my book, which was never written. Time passed, and many people checked in later, asking, "How's the book coming along?" or "Have you finished your book yet?" I succumbed to the quick death of my shallowly rooted reality by answering, "It's not," and "No I have not."

You see, announcing all my intentions quickly garnered the praise and attention of actually having done it without having done a single thing. I realized that my mouth was a credit card that appeared to have a limitless line of credit. Therefore, week after week, year after year, I swiped that card, charging up a hefty debt of "gonna-do's" yet not making a single payment on the transactions my mouth had made. In the words of neo-soul singer Musiq Soulchild, "All that shoulda woulda coulda don't mean nothin'."[5] The bill becomes due. *The bill always becomes due.* Like the proverbial irresponsible teenager given his or her first credit card, I spent recklessly. I frequently missed payments: I announced what I was doing and got the praise and attention for having done it. *Swipe.* But when people checked in later and asked how things were coming along, I had nothing to show for it and no updates. *Missed payment.* In real life, when you continue to charge a credit card and not make payments, banks and credit-card companies will choose not to loan you money in the future, and they'll eventually close your account. All my announcements eventually led to me losing "credit" (credibility) with people, and my grand announcements no longer meant as much. They were once met with excitement and critical acclaim, but now, they were met with doubt and suspicion. I know that many of my friends felt like saying, "Jay T., I'll believe it when I see it." I could feel the sun setting on my big dreams and ideas. The excitement of it all slowed down and drew its final breaths as I progressed toward inactivity. The darkness encroached. The heart monitor that just a few weeks/months ago was racing at a rapid pace, beeping melodically vibrant, now slowed down completely. The line flattened until it was completely horizontal. No change. No heartbeat. No life. Only death.

I could liken it to eating candy for breakfast when in need of energy and a pick-me-up. Oh, it's so tasty, so sweet, and immediately satisfying, but the carbohydrates in candy are empty sugars that only provide energy for a moment. Because they lack substantial nutrition, once our metabolisms burn through those sugars, we are left with a crash afterward. We are quickly high and then we quickly crash. Announcing my moves was a quick high but was always accompanied by an immediate crash. The quick sprout of praise for announcing, "I'm going to do a CD and release music!" was followed by the drastic crash of responding to the follow-up question about the progress—"I haven't started yet. It's not done yet. Nothing." ***I came to the end of myself, realizing I wanted attention more than I wanted success.*** I wanted to be seen more than I wanted the realization of my goals.

2.1 A Reckless Sower

In keeping with the parable of the sower, I was forced to a few difficult revelations as I continued to see myself in this text:

> And He spoke many things to them in parables, saying, "Behold, the sower went out to sow; and as he sowed, some seeds fell beside the road, and the birds came and ate them up. Others fell on rocky places, where they did not have much soil; and immediately they sprang up, because they had no depth of soil. But when the sun had risen, they were scorched; and because they had no root, they withered away. Others fell among the thorns, and the thorns came up and choked them out. And others fell on the good soil and yielded a crop, some a hundredfold, some sixty, and some thirty. He who has ears, let him hear Matthew 13:1-9 (New American Standard Bible).

This pericope chiefly deals with hearing and understanding the Word of the Kingdom of God and how various forces of life try to stifle, kill, and obstruct the understanding of the kingdom message. The result of these forces is ultimately to keep people from accepting the message of the Kingdom, a realm of good news for all. I previously identified myself with the seed sown on rocky ground with shallow soil, but I realized I had much more to bear with this text than rocky ground. God Almighty had deposited ideas and dreams within me, and the Creator wanted me to create. As I quickly began telling people all that was in my head, while searching for praise and recognition, I shared my ideas with just about anyone who would listen. I dropped my seeds virtually anywhere. In doing so, I look back, now, and see that I had left my seeds/ideas in places where birds had come to eat them up. It is interesting that in this parable, it is birds that come to snatch away the seed and devour it. Birds can have a unique meaning, especially in the context of American colloquialisms. You've heard the phrase "I heard from a little bird that . . ." and immediately the conversation turns to gossip. "A little bird told me that . . ." and you can be assured that you'll be told about someone else's business, whether it's fact or fiction. Those birds surely know how to gossip and run their mouths. The birds in the text ate the seed; it was destroyed and could never take root because of them. I failed to realize that as I spread my seed to the "birds" in the same manner, my dreams could never take root because some of the people, who heard me carelessly go on and on, honestly, couldn't have cared less. I discovered later that many of them envied me and turned to criticism and gossip rather than celebrating me—ultimately, to destroy the seed.

Why do people become jealous? Perhaps it's because you represent something they want to do or be. It could also be because they are comparing themselves to you. That's why they follow you on social media and quietly keep tabs on you. This is part of a social phenomenon called Social Comparison, which I'll delve into more in a later chapter.

I arrived at the rude awakening that, in this world, not everybody will like you. Just because they smile in your face and act cordial and friendly does not mean they are indeed your friend. My naïveté washed away the more this happened to me. If you cannot support me or allow me to support you, celebrate me, create with me, build with me, produce with me—then you cannot possibly be my friend. That is not what a friend is or what a friend does. I gave too many seeds to jealous, envious, gossiping birds of Cain (Genesis 4:1–18).

Next, as previously mentioned, I had sown plenty of seeds in rocky places. My first response to each new idea was to announce it before putting any roots down to allow a plan to develop toward actualizing it. Of course, they sprang up quickly! Who would believe I was blatantly lying when I said, "I'll have a book coming out soon"? They knew I had a lot to say and that I have strong opinions, but, ultimately, it all lacked deep roots. The roots were shallow and superficial, at best. Announcing my plans was the product of short roots in shallow soil, but this revealed a deeply rooted issue within my heart that needed to be addressed for the sake of my emotional health and future. I craved attention, and I gladly reaped the rewards as I boasted my various "I'm gonna's." I was desperate for affirmation. There was a void in my heart that sought to fill itself with attention and affirmation because there were false beliefs, deep down on the inside, to which I subscribed: I'm not good enough, and nobody cares about me. When asked what his greatest regret was, Bishop T.D. Jakes answered that he most regretted not believing in himself enough. I struggle with believing in myself and realizing my potential. I still wrestle with that "you're not good enough" lie and fight daily to overcome it and to accept the truths about myself instead of the lies. I am good enough. I am capable. I am accepted. I am loved. I am cherished. I am safe. I have a home. I have a place to where I belong. I am known by name by God. These are powerful and true declarations. Won't you take a moment to verbalize these confessions yourself?

I am good enough.

I am capable.

I am accepted.

I am loved.

I am cherished.

I am safe.

I have a home.

I have a place to where I belong.

I am known by name by God.

2.2 Working for My Good

I have a God who loves me so much that He sent His only son to die for me. I am valued by the Lord so much that He invests a measure of His own

Spirit within me to lead me to greatness and to bring out all the good things He Himself placed within me. He sees my worth, and because of that, He prunes me. He allows the rain and the sun because they are both part of the "all things" that work together for my good. The sun should be a good thing, conducive for my growth and development, but in the absence of deep roots, it scorches and burns away the growth of my seed. There were "suns" in my life—people who were there to help better me and guide me toward my success. Their light, life, and influence surely would have helped me grow in every area, but because I lacked the depth, I ultimately wasn't ready for their light. I was more concerned about growing out than I was growing down to develop my roots—to shine for a fleeting moment rather than be established for a lifetime. A professor at Ashland Theological Seminary once explained the phenomenon of trees that grow in the desert. How on earth could a tree or any vegetation sprout up in the desert? The sun is hot, and a water source can seem so far away that it would be impossible for any plant to survive. But trees do survive and flourish even in a desert. This is not due to their proximity to water, but beneath the surface, their roots stretch, reaching for miles at a time until they tap into a water source. Once connected with water, the rest is history.

I matured and realized that the most important thing was for me to have deeply established roots that always connected me to my source, Christ Jesus. What is your source? What are you connected to? As long as I'm connected to the source no matter what happens in this life, no matter how inclement the conditions, no matter how severe the storm, no matter how arid the desert, I'll survive and flourish in spite of it all. I'm thankful for the roots and even more thankful for the source!

There is so much more to be said about the criticality of having established roots and connections as well as the time and dedication to grow proper roots. Remember, we must grow down before we grow up. We must be fastened and secured to a higher power to survive. I believe an old hymn said it best: "There's a storm out over the ocean, and it's moving this old way. If your soul is not anchored in Jesus, it will surely drift away. If your soul is not anchored in Jesus, it will surely drift away."[6]

2.3 Intentions and Declarations

One would think that to make your intentions known that it would create an atmosphere of accountability. Some argue that publicly stating a behavioral intention would commit you to a certain self-view. For example stating, "I am a reliable person." The follow-up behaviors are things like promptly answering every phone call that hits your cell phone and readily availing yourself to others at all times. It sounds logical that the result of letting people know what you intend to do would be a surefire way to goal completion. The pressure of them knowing and anticipating the completion of your intentions gets behind you like a cheerleader and coaches you on to the end. But does it really?

The self-completion theory proposes that people who are committed to identity goals can embark on several activities to attain those goals. For example, a person with an identity goal to be a music artist will undertake activities such as singing karaoke, securing public performances, songwriting, or recording a CD to establish his- or herself as a music artist. These activities are known as identity symbols in the world of behavioral psychology. If I am a medical doctor or desire to become one, some of my identity symbols may include going to medical school, conducting tests in a lab, and performing surgeries in the operating room. Research has shown, however, that failing to engage in one of the identity-symbol activities or not having one at all produces a state of feeling incomplete.[7] Again, you can't stand still, but you have to do something in line with whatever you want to be. To make up for this feeling of incompleteness, the person must now locate and engage in other identity symbols. Simply put, you have to be something else now and quickly figure out what it is because you're on a journey to define who you are. Along these lines, here are two things that research in self-completion theory reveals that highly pertain to *HushAndDo*. One, when an individual's identity symbols (activities corresponding to the identity goals) are noticed by a social audience, the result is that he or she reaches a higher level of completeness. Two, incomplete individuals are more concerned with finding an audience for their identity strivings, compared with complete individuals.[8] This sounds a lot like the person I used to be. How about you?

Peter M. Gollwitzer, a leading psychologist in the field of self-completion theory and studies related to goal completion, motivation, and behavior, conducted a study with college students aspiring to be psychologists. The participants were informed that they would take part in a survey about the study intentions of first-year psychology students. They were first asked questions regarding their commitment to becoming psychologists. Next, the students were asked to write down their two most important study intentions for the upcoming week. For example, "I'm going to read fifty pages of psychology literature every day," or "I'm going to exclusively study for sixty additional minutes each day on top of my normal study regimen." The group was divided into two sections. Under the guise of making sure the students understood the survey, the experimenter read each student's study intentions to the first group, which was the social-reality group. He was, in fact, acknowledging each student's intentions not only to himself but also to the entire room. Thus, the social reality was created—attention and recognition for declared intentions. In the other group, the nonsocial-reality group, the students were informed that their study-intentions lists were a mistake and shouldn't be included in the survey. They could simply keep them for themselves or throw them away. Therefore, the students' study intentions were unacknowledged and unnoticed—no attention and no recognition. A week later, all participants were sent a second questionnaire that asked them to restate their study intentions as well as record the days and times that they acted upon them. The results of this study showed that the social-reality group (the group whose study intentions were acknowledged) actually acted upon their intentions far less than the unacknowledged group. The nonsocial-reality group did more of what they said they intended to do than the social-reality group!

A similar study was conducted shortly afterward, this time with law students. As before, they were introduced to a questionnaire that asked about their commitment to studying and practicing law. The central statement was, "I intend to make the best possible use of educational opportunities in law." In the social-reality group, the experimenter verified the student's responses individually, confirming that they were sure of the response they chose. In the nonsocial-reality group, the students simply turned in their anonymous questionnaires without reviewing the answers with the experimenter. In the second part of the study, the students were asked to sort through twenty different criminal law cases to find those acceptable to develop a computer-based study-package for future law students. They were all given 45 minutes to finish the case they were working on, and when the 45-minute mark arrived, they were given extra time. They were also given the option to finish earlier if they so desired. As you can probably guess, the students whose intentions were acknowledged in the beginning more often ended their reviews of the cases early and overall did less work than the unacknowledged group. Are you beginning to see the trend?

Gollwitzer and his associates conducted two more similar studies, dividing a social-reality group from a nonsocial-reality group. Though the methods varied in each study, the results ran concurrently through all four studies. From these studies, they concluded that when intentions are acknowledged by a social group, the performance of the declared intentions is decreased and compromised. Other people who take notice of one's identity-relevant intentions apparently engenders a premature sense of completeness regarding the identity goal.[9] When people acknowledge you for the things you seek to be and do, it's as if you've already completed all the related tasks toward those said intentions and have magically fast-forwarded to the finish line of success. The acknowledgment makes you feel successful. It quenches a desire for identity and social esteem (what others think of you) within you. These feelings can be described by a myriad of adjectives. However, we must remember that they are just feelings, and feelings don't translate to the hard work it takes to follow through and finish strong.

It's wonderful to have vast dreams and aspirations. Think greater. Expand the capacity of your mind to dream loftily. Take the limits off, and go! Years ago, a friend told me it was indeed okay to dream; however, to continually dream but commit no action toward it, is no longer a dream but a hallucination. You have to be hallucinating to believe dreams can be achieved with no work and no plan. This is why it's paramount to major in your HUSH before you major in your DO.

2.4 The Inward Journey Goes Deeper

Honestly, do you just want attention, or do you want to fulfill your goals? Be forthright with yourself and assess where you are currently. If your honesty reveals that you desire attention and recognition more than anything, then let's chase that by asking why. Then, let's chase it further away by digging in to reveal the deep wounds in your life.

I had to be transparent with myself and address the various layers of pain, lies, dysfunctional behavior, and deep wounds that had affected my life situation and that drove my need for attention and affirmation. Most of what follows stands on the shoulders of a significant influence in my life: Dr. Terry Wardle, my former seminary professor at Ashland Theological Seminary.

Earlier in this chapter, I mentioned some false beliefs to which I subscribed. These include, but aren't limited to, "I'm not good enough; nobody cares; and what I say and do has no significance." There are many more with which I wrestle and renounce, but I'll focus on these. Those false beliefs, also referred to as lies and distortions, form just one layer of several in emotional difficulty, which Wardle likens to an onion.[10] For now, let's move from this layer to the outermost layer and work our way to the core.

It begins at my life's situation, the place where I experienced pain and difficulty. I was a frustrated, exhausted, and disappointed minister, worship leader, and musician who always knew my career would be unique—a line of work for which one couldn't apply and send a résumé and cover letter but whose doors would have to be opened by God. I am grateful He has trusted me to do what I love, to do it for His glory, and earn a decent income as a result. I was frustrated because I had so many creative ideas flowing through my head all the time yet could rarely get them to translate into business practices and ministry moves. I was exhausted because for some reason, which we'll soon discover, it completely drained my energy to focus and finish whatever I started no matter how big or how small. I was disappointed because I often shared these ideas yet the vast majority of them never materialized. I was leaving loads of potential in a state of potential, rarely translating them to kinetic activity and completion. Beneath this outermost layer is dysfunctional behavior, the unhealthy ways I coped with my life. I shared my ideas with virtually anyone who would listen. I ran from person to person searching for attention, affirmation, and applause. Under this layer was an emotional upheaval, feelings I experienced regularly that drove me to the dysfunctional behaviors.

These included feeling lonely as if nobody understood me—feeling abandoned, depressed, and like a constant disappointment. I, Jay T. Hairston II, with all my charisma, charm, and many talents, could barely get anything done. So that meant hundreds, if not thousands, of yearning people needed competent ministry, and I wasn't producing anything. Therefore, I was letting them down and, ultimately, my God. Does that sound at all truthful? Sadly, I believe it does to countless others in ministry who sense a call to help people.

But this is a lie. This is also the layer preceding emotional upheaval where I began this section, false beliefs. Past this layer, we arrive at the painful core that set everything in motion, deep wounding. We all have areas in our life where we have been wounded, and it takes many shapes. For me, the wounds are things that have been spoken to me throughout my life. Regardless of the intention, some people's words cut me deeply. I was always being challenged to do better even after I had given my absolute best. In addition, being a young minister, who sincerely loved the Lord, and a young man, who had dedicated his life to God, raised everyone's expectations of me. Whenever I did anything that didn't quite resemble the perfect appearance of a pastor or a seasoned minister, I was called out and criticized by both friends and family. That created a strong pressure that made me feel like I needed to perform well and meet others' expectations my entire life. People were watching and waiting for my success, and I couldn't disappoint them. I had to do well. I was a husky child, or as some would say, big-boned. The truth is, my bones were perfectly normal. They just had a lot of meat wrapped around them! (It's okay to laugh at that . . . we're in this thing together, and I know how to laugh at myself! Haha!)

Hearing things like, "You're a handsome young man, but now let's get this weight off you, and you'll look even more handsome," translated to me as, "You're almost handsome but not quite." These words and similar instances pierced my heart and soul. I was deeply wounded and needed to medicate the pain. Do you see how this emotional onion works its way inside and back out? These painful words immediately led me to believe I wasn't good enough and had to perform at a certain level to win the affection and approval of people and God. As a result, I often felt unsatisfied and was seldom pleased with anything I did. Nobody could understand the pressure and responsibility to perform and to not compromise my witness for the Lord. I felt responsible for the well-being of other's souls. This also was a distorted lie. Struggling to be a *good guy* feeling like the eyes of my entire community were constantly upon me, I still searched for validation. It was dysfunctional to always seek affirmation from others, fishing for compliments and positive reinforcement. This pursuit to restore my broken emotions—and for one day feel good about myself—took precedence over recording my CD, writing sermons, writing books, my work, and even my ministry. I told myself that I wanted to get all of that done, but the truth was, more than completing those projects, my heart really longed for attention and affirmation. This is why I was often frustrated, exhausted, and disappointed. Not only was I failing to advance in my work and produce that which was in me, but also, those in whom I confided failed to provide the nurturing I was looking for, and if they did, it was never enough. I was never satisfied and always needed more. I was looking to exhaustive and incomplete sources to do something that only the Inexhaustible One could do. I know I'm not the only one who has dealt with this, and it's my hope that my transparency can help you be even more honest with yourself, especially if this is you.

There is healing for the deep wounding in your soul. You do not have to be a prisoner of negative emotions, dysfunctional behaviors, and pain. There is freedom. Here my faith and theology will take the lead for this portion of our journey. I can think of no greater healer than Jesus the Christ. In *Healing Care, Healing Prayer*, Wardle provides a structure for prayer to position ourselves for healing and liberation[11]: The Holy Spirit is ever present and ever ready to minister to your wounds and heal you. He just needs our invitation and attention. God entrusted the management of all things on Earth to mankind (Genesis 1). Therefore, God needs our invitation to divinely intervene in the earth and humanity. He needs our attention because He has already been preparing for this moment and how to help you move forward after the hurt. He knows what you need, and *He knows best.* He's ready to meet you in the places of your pain and heal you. I identify two essential statements within the Gospel of John that guide my conviction concerning what our response to God should be in this context. The religious elite took issue with Jesus healing a man who was lame in John 5, claiming He was doing work on the Sabbath and that wasn't permitted. This happened much to the chagrin of these religious quacks, as they were hung up on Jesus' *work* and not the man's *miracle.* Jesus responded by saying, "My Father is working until now, and I Myself am working" John 5:17 (NASB). The finale of John's gospel bears the second essential statement, "And there are also many other things which Jesus did, which if they were written in detail, I suppose that even the world itself would not contain the books that would be written" John 21:25 (NASB). The world they knew in first-century Palestine wouldn't have been able to contain the books that would have been written about the acts of Jesus Christ. He did so much in His lifetime, most of which came from His three-year public ministry, that there wouldn't be enough pages to write them all down—all this, in just a brief moment in time. Juxtapose that to the first essential statement in which Jesus said that the Father is still working even until now. The Father has been working before time began, since time's inception, throughout time, until this present moment, and will continue to work afterward. If the world couldn't contain the pages of His acts in the brief stint of Jesus' life, imagine just how overwhelming it would be to even imagine the number of pages it would take to record the activity of God since time began! How uncontainable, therefore, would it be to detail all that Jesus has been doing in the 2000-plus years since His resurrection? I'd venture to say there wouldn't be enough trees on this planet to produce enough paper to begin to write down even half of what He's done! The Father is working. He's busy. So many people preoccupy themselves by trying to figure things out for themselves, but it's futile. I surmise that your busyness should be that of paying attention to the One who's been busy, our Creator. Let's invite His participation into our midst and quiet ourselves that we may discern where He would like to take things once we're before Him.

The moment you are with God is like none other. He knows how to speak in a clear and gentle way—a way you can understand. I encourage you to have honest conversations with God about how you're feeling and what has happened. Tell Him how you feel about the people who wounded you and as well as God Himself. Perhaps He's the object of your anger and disappointment. The painful event(s) in your life happened, and God, for some reason, didn't stop it. Grapple with those feelings and with God. I promise you, the Father is not nearly as fragile, petty, and peevish as we tend to make Him. He can take your deepest and darkest secrets, hold on to them, and not tell a soul. He takes the worst news and feelings right on the chin and doesn't even flinch. Even for those of us who are more down to earth than others, some things we could hear would make us gasp or scrunch our faces. However, God takes the most ominous news, the inmost feelings, and His face doesn't change one bit. In spite of it all, He still listens, ready to respond with comforting words and healing, yet He's patient enough to let you talk it out, vent, and grieve completely.

What a friend we have in Jesus. Embark on this inward journey to self-discovery and healing. After spending time in His healing presence, you'll be able to renounce the lies in your life and replace your distorted beliefs with truth. This truth gives us comfort and peace in the place of the negative emotional upheavals you previously experienced. Your living will be empowered as you stand on God's promises instead of Satan's lies, which changes the way you behave from dysfunctional to functional and healthy, and, ultimately, it will impact your life.

I realize I quickly laid out a path to emotional wellness. Please know that this path is a process that will require time and consistency. ***Every purpose has a process.*** This won't be an overnight change, but your process can begin immediately.

Allow me to share an image I have used for this type of prayer and healing. It has helped me move forward and get healing in many areas. I'm sure you've seen the proverbial hostage crisis-situation in a movie. There's always that one police officer, detective, or FBI agent, who's ready to jump the gun and rush in with brute force and strength, unwilling to negotiate with the captor. Usually, he is paired with the overcautious colleague who doesn't want to move to brash action and takes a more systematic and calculated approach. Their tension throughout the crisis is palpable and both gain support from us, the viewers, during the entire ordeal. Most importantly, either side can't make a move until the head detective or police chief gives the go-ahead. The SWAT team surrounds the building, ready to storm in where the hostages are being held. The snipers are in view on top of the roofs of nearby buildings, waiting for any appearance of the captor or any of his henchmen to take them down. The bystanders are outside praying and anxiously awaiting the good news that the hostages were freed and that nobody was lost. We all watch in animated suspense until the climactic moment where the man in charge says, "Move in!" Everyone springs into action.

Imagine that your heart, soul, mind, and body are the building where the hostages are being held. The hostages in your heart aren't physical people but your joy, your peace, your safety and security, your happiness, etc. How long have you gone without any of these? It's definitely time to be restored and made whole. The captor is the enemy who came in and wounded your heart using whatever took place in your life to break your soul. His henchmen helping them keep the hostages bound are the lies and distortions these deep wounds have caused.

The brute-force cop represents the emotions that want to quickly end the pain and move forward. You're fed up with being bound and hurt.

You're desperate for a change and for the pain in your heart to stop. The cautious cop represents another set of emotions—fear. You're afraid of moving forward too quickly due to potential backlash and the possibility of reliving painful memories and revisiting some harrowing places from your past as you grieve the loss that the deep wound created. You're afraid of confronting the pain of your past, but you must in order to move forward and walk in healing. The bystanders outside consist of your family, friends, and loved ones who want to see you free and healthy. They are praying for you and awaiting the news that your process of healing has begun and that the captor is eliminated. The SWAT team surrounding the building is the Holy Spirit with the Lord's angels, anxiously awaiting the go-ahead command from you—the man/woman in charge, authorized to give the command. I promise you, He can heal the wounded areas and restore your soul if given permission.

If you'd like to, you can pray this model prayer with me:

Heavenly Father,

I confess my feelings regarding

____

(whatever happened to you).

It made me feel like

____

and as a result, I felt feelings of

____

I now make the choice to trust You, and I give Your heavenly SWAT team permission to invade my soul. Please come into my heart, mind, and soul and search the entire building, which is me. Sweep through the place, and as soon as You locate the captor and his henchmen, please eliminate them. After You've eliminated them from my soul, then please set all the captives free.

Set free my joy, my peace, my security, my confidence, my happiness, and hope that they can once again live unhindered and unencumbered here in the residence of your temple, my body. Please stay with me and keep guard, day and night, that the evildoers may not return. Your protection will give me peace and comfort. Lastly, if You find anything that should not be, please remove it and replace it only with the things You declare should be there.

Holy Spirit, You have my permission to do Your work in my heart, and I will try not to interrupt you. Please come in immediately and do what only You can do.

In Jesus' name, amen.

May this chapter be the gentle door opening your heart to allow you to be real with yourself, and please continue to examine your life as you continue reading.

Thank you for taking this courageous step on the journey with me.

Chapter 3

Fear—The Only Way Past Is Through

Jesus said, "Oh Peter, Peter don't be afraid.

Jesus said, "Oh Peter, don't be afraid.

Jesus said, "Oh Peter, don't be afraid.

Walk on the water. Walk on the water. Walk on the water.

Peter, don't be afraid.[12]

How I desperately wish the Soul Stirrers had replaced the name Peter with my name, Jay T., and dedicated this song to me each time I had the lucky draw to be the organist for Dr. R.A. Vernon as he preached to thousands at The Word Church in Cleveland, Ohio.

I'm going to share one of my many stories of fear in hopes that it will encourage you and perhaps give you a few lighthearted laughs as well.

3.1 Backing Him Up: Something I Completely Dreaded

Preaching and music are arguably the two most critical hallmarks of the Black Church experience. When looking for a church home, most congregants look for a good preached Word and great music and singing. The preacher uses combinations of four devices to present her or his message: pitch, pace, pause, and volume. In addition, my grandfather always told me preaching in the Black Church involved three main elements to be successful: the preacher, the audience (their response and participation in the message), and the Holy Spirit. A fourth element is introduced only when the first three have been met; a technique called whooping. Notable Black preachers such as C. L. Franklin, Jasper Williams, Jr., and Dr. Caesar Clark used this whooping style most prevalently. Whooping is when the preacher combines his or her message with music, usually toward the end of their sermon.

It's closing out the homily with singing instead of normal speech delivery. This is usually accompanied by an organist. As the preacher starts the whoop, unless pre-discussed before the presentation, the organist must quickly locate whatever key the preacher is in and use chords of the same key to back up the preacher. She will say something in tune, and during her brief pause between statements/whooping, the organist will jump in and just as briefly play a corresponding chord. This organic flow of back-and-forth between preacher and organist can go on for as little as one minute to well over ten minutes! It's like playing jump rope: the two people twirling the two ropes are the preacher and the organist—the person who is trying to perfectly time when to jump in. I've had the privilege to be both twirler and jumper, but I'd rather be the twirler any day! Now that you've had a brief lesson on preaching in the Black Church tradition, we can return to my story about fear.

I am a singer, a musician, a choir director, and a preacher. I tend to lean toward preaching and singing, yet I embrace all of my gifts and enjoy operating in each of them. It's imperative that there is always a musician on the organ ready to back up Dr. Vernon at The Word Church. There are so many wonderful keyboard players and organists on staff who I believe could play circles around me. Don't get me wrong, I can surely hold my own, and there was a reason I was initially hired as a musician; however, these brothers run mightily in this particular lane of music performance. I would default to any of the other organists any time the opportunity arose to back up Dr. Vernon on the organ. The truth is that I wasn't providing the other guys a wonderful opportunity to accompany the pastor, but really, I was avoiding one of my biggest fears. That was my cover-up.

I have a deep love and respect for Dr. Vernon dating back to my late-teenage years. His name was so frequently mentioned in Cleveland that before long I took it upon myself, a seventeen-year-old high-school junior, to visit The Word Church just to see what all the hoopla was truly about. Then I would return to the West Side suburbs of Cleveland where I lived to give the religious community of color there either the thumbs-up or thumbs-down about this man and this church. Now, looking back, I laugh at myself and my manner of thinking back then. Really, just *who was I* to appraise, assess and affirm his validity and authenticity to my community? I was just a kid! I came. I saw. I recognized. God was really with that man, still is, and his heart to love the Lord and to love people was most sincere. It rivaled that of my own. From that day forward, he had and *always will* have my love, respect, and support. My strong conviction and emotion for this man and his church accompany me every time I set foot in the building, and especially every time the lot fell upon me to back him up on the organ.

I have a high level of honor for good music, good preaching, and for Dr. Vernon. These three created a seemingly insurmountable wall of anxiety for me when it was time to back him up—a man, a church, and a message, I love so deeply and hold to be sacred.

What if I didn't play that well behind him? What if I broke his cadence and rhythm? That would interfere with the Word going forth that the people so desperately needed. If someone came to church that day and missed a fresh Word from heaven because of a mistake I made on the organ, I could never live with myself. That was seriously my train of thought and how sincerely I venerated my role. Add that to the fact that I was not confident in my playing ability. I grew up in a mixed Black, Latino, and White charismatic church, and our Puerto Rican pastor wasn't a whooper. I didn't grow up in this style of church and preaching, similar to my colleagues. I knew the chord sequence and structure to back up a preacher, and have done it plenty of times before, but this was different.

Therefore, my self-appointed role and coping mechanism were to AVOID GETTING ON THAT ORGAN AT ALL COSTS. To save face, I would hover nearby and give advice to anybody on the organ, especially if they were newer to the church and to Dr. Vernon's preaching style. Destiny would have it that one Sunday, all the musicians were unavailable. I alone remained in Akron, Ohio, the last line of defense for the music ministry to back up Dr. Vernon. I begged and pleaded with my supervisor, Mark Jackson, offering to take his place and head back to the main location for the next service, and he could stay and finish service with the pastor. After thirty seconds of failed negotiation and reasoning with my dear friend, or so I thought, he left me—helpless and afraid, all alone to confront this colossal task to be the organist during the sermon. The man LEFT ME!

I took my seat on that wooden organ bench before a thousand people in the audience while Pastor Vernon had already begun preaching. I panned the audience with all of my might, hoping I would locate a musician there and could surely get him to run up on stage and take my place on the old rugged cross. Nobody was there but me. My stomach churned and sank as low as it could go. Alas, a sudden bathroom emergency could save me from my terror, but no, I couldn't come down from that tree. My head was now covered in a nervous sweat. The praise team sitting nearby behind the stage looked at me puzzled about why I was so fidgety and uncomfortable. They knew me as a musician, but they didn't know I wasn't confident in myself at all! My eyes were sweating. Yes, it was sweat, and it came from my eyes. My heart raced through my chest. My hands shook like learning to drive a stick shift. How could I play a single chord if they were shaking worse than a broken washing machine? I set my drawbars and got everything in position. Fortunately, Dr. Vernon has a few phrases he often used, and those were clear signals for when he wanted you to chime in behind him.

He hit his first catchphrase, "High-five ten people, and say, 'I feel that!' " and I hit him quickly (which means I played chords behind that and did a rift directly afterward). He kept preaching! I thought the run was pretty smooth and successful. I actually impressed myself. He didn't look back, so it must have been okay. Minutes later another phrase, "Stand up, and sit back down, and say, 'God did it!' " and I hit him yet again, embellishing a little more this time as my wavering confidence began to sprout. A few more key phrases roared across the podium, and I cleanly filled the gap. I was feeling pretty good. We were getting to the end of the message, and I thought, *Perhaps today I'd get lucky, and he wouldn't go into a full whoop but just teach calmly with some occasional expression.* That was my best bet! That fateful Akron Sunday, he came not only to teach but also to preach, armed with a complete and thorough whoop, *locked, loaded, and ready to fire*! This moment was one of my biggest fears, and it was manifesting before my very eyes. At this point, there was no way to escape. The only way to get *over* it was to go *through it.*

I don't care if you're reading this alone in your room right now; you need to find five people and high-five them and say, "The only way to get over it is to go through it!"

He hit what would be his last phrase before his whoop started, "Why don't you take thirty seconds and praise Him!" I hit him again and provided enough accompaniment to the last thirty seconds. Toward the end of what felt like a lifetime, I played another riff that remarkably blew my own mind. As soon as I finished it, I hollered out, "Whew!" amazed that I was really doing this! As soon as I said "Whew!" Dr. Vernon said, "Yes!" He looked back at me, smiled, and thus the whoop began. I pushed him there. There's no turning back now! At this point, it's all-in. All the drawbars are pulled out for a fuller sound, and I wouldn't lift my fingers from the organ until he was done. My confidence burst through the fear as I kept backing him up. The audience was receiving not only the word but the Spirit-filled moment as well. Soon the drummer would join me, Chef Marcus Tate, and it was just the two of us with Dr. Vernon closing out the service with a rocking hallelujah good time.

Conquering the fear released my inhibitions, and I played that organ freely and fully, even matching the very tune of each word he whooped. I felt like I was sitting on top of the world brimming with courage and fearlessness to serve my church in this critical capacity. I was winning . . . until he modulated a half step up to E major. (Gospel musicians will find the humor in this.) Oh, don't worry. I had him in the key of E too! Perhaps next time we can just stay in E-flat. Please?

3.2 The Only Way Over Is Through

For so long, and for so many, fear has been like an armed bodyguard standing at the door of your goals and aspirations, keeping you out each time you try to get in. It has kept so many of us paralyzed, including myself. Fear varies in the forms it takes with each of us, yet we are all connected in the sense that in one way or another, one day or the next, we will experience, and have all experienced, fear. My goal is to transform your thinking about fear. For however long it's blocked you, fear has rendered you helpless and barred you from purpose. I want to show you that fear is not the burly bouncer standing in front of the door, ***but it is the door, and the only way to get past it—is to go through it***.

Dr. Susan Jeffers breaks down fear into three levels, starting at a surface level and traveling inward.[13] Level-One fears are broken into two categories: things that happen and things that require action. Examples of the first would be the fear of dying, aging, becoming disabled, or natural disasters, to name a few. They are all things that can occur. The second can include things like going back to school, losing weight, making friends, and finding love. These are all things that require action to happen. Level-Two fears run a little deeper than the first level, as they are not situation-oriented, but they involve our heart, soul, and our ego. Examples of these can include fear of rejection, failure (which is a big one for me), and being vulnerable. This level impacts the first level because it begins internally within your mind and then proceeds externally. A fear of failure, which is internal, feeds your fear of potentially losing your job, which is external and can happen to any of us. As a result of the fear of failure, you shy away from the doors that could open to amazing opportunities that could open amazing doors in your life. You're reluctant to take risks because you fear failing. It's unfortunate because success requires a certain degree of risk-taking. Level-Three gets to the root of all the fears located within the first two levels: "I can't handle it!"[14] That seems basic, but this is what it all boils down to that we cannot handle what life throws at us.

Use me as an illustration of how this works. At the first level that requires action, I feared backing up the preacher on the organ during a live church service. At the second internal level, I feared that making mistakes would ruin the entire church service. I ultimately feared that I couldn't handle making a mistake. I thought it would literally be impossible to handle what would happen if I made mistakes because it was impossible for me to know how Dr. Vernon or the audience would respond. The element of the unknown threatened me. I didn't know whether I would be fired, relieved of organ duties, given a stern lecture after service, or even possibly have blood on my hands for the soul that came to receive the Word and couldn't because I got in the way. Some of these fears produced false beliefs to which I subscribed. Am I really single-handedly responsible for a congregant's reception of the preached word? I am not, but my fear drove me to believe this. Regardless of the appearance of the fear and whatever emotions it triggers within you, there remains a path forward and, sequentially, through.

3.3 Habituation and Exposure: The Way Through

We are programmed to recognize fear and respond to it as a method of survival from physical danger. This is traditionally known as the fight-or-flight response. During the onset of a threat, fear, or stress, three main hormones (among many others) are released as we encounter a threatening or stressful stimulus: adrenaline, norepinephrine, and cortisol. The irony is that our bodies don't know how to distinguish between physical threats from emotional ones. The same hormones are released whether I'm being held at gunpoint or I have to sit in behind the preacher. The adrenaline release gives us a surge of energy. Norepinephrine helps us to be more aware, awake, and focused. Cortisol takes a little longer to release, but when it finally does, it helps regulate blood pressure and fluid balance. This all happens in our bodies whether we're in imminent physical danger or if we are considering that thing of which we are afraid. They both trigger these hormonal responses. Fear has a way of conflating itself to larger-than-life proportions in many circumstances, especially considering how our bodies cannot differentiate between the two. However, most psychologists conclude that one of the most effective ways to address fear is exposure and exposure therapy.

It's cliché, but it's true that we must face our fears to get past them. We must be exposed to them. In that exposure, we find out that the thing we feared, and its threat, isn't as great as we thought it was. More importantly, the fear's threat doesn't increase, becoming more *dangerous,* while we're in its presence. Once I engaged it, I discovered that my fear to back up the preacher didn't escalate indefinitely. The *threat* was the same *threat* it had always been. Nothing changed. What exposure does is remarkable, and it tears down some of fear's lies. The aim of exposure is to reduce your fear response by means of extinction learning.[15] This happens when we are repeatedly exposed to the thing that makes us afraid, yet during that time of exposure, there are no negative consequences. Thus, we begin to associate the thing we're afraid of with feelings of relative safety because nothing bad had happened when we confronted it. In that brief Sunday morning moment, that seemed like a month of Sundays, the longer I was in it and each time I successfully played behind him, the more my narrative changed about backing him up. There in that moment, feelings of despair and panic had transformed into feelings of pride and satisfaction as I actually began to enjoy the moment and myself. I could tolerate it long enough until nonthreatening associations began to form. I positively reinforced myself to keep playing behind him and, as a result, the fear lessened more and more. This is an example of the mechanism of habituation. Habituation, defined formally, refers to the fact that nervous system arousal decreases on repeated exposure to the same stimulus.[16] What it really means is that familiar things get boring to us because we are exposed to them repeatedly. When we habituate familiar things, instead of focusing our energies on the familiar thing, we now can direct more energy toward novel stimuli.

When I was teaching my daughter her ABCs, we began with one letter at a time, starting with the letter B because her name is Brooklyn. Every day we explored words with the letter B and reinforced that letter daily. Every time she saw the B, initially she would jump and down with excitement. After a while, she got used to seeing the letter B, and it wasn't met with the same toddler energy as when we first introduced it. The time finally came to move on to the letter C. As soon as she saw it, you could see the lights turn on in her mind. "Ah, something new! Yay!" She now directed her energy to the letter C and her rejoicing returned with the introduction of the new letter. Bye B!

I use habituation to help the singers I train in my choirs and ensembles to overcome stage fright. Singing before others, whether peers or strangers, can be a daunting task for someone who has never done it before. I start small and have them practice singing in front of a small audience first, their fellow choir members or praise team members, in the safe context of a rehearsal setting. They don't normally sing in front of others due to their fear, which is the fear that they can't handle how others will respond to their singing; therefore, it remains a new stimulus. As a result, each time he or she has to sing in front of others, the body will still release adrenaline, norepinephrine, and cortisol and engage in flight-or-fight mode.

Fortunately, as each rehearsal goes by and we keep at it, singing before one's peers becomes a habit. It becomes normal. As it normalizes, it's no longer a novel stimulus, and as a result, with each repeated instance of facing that fear, the body reacts less and less to it, therefore, not releasing the same amounts of adrenaline, norepinephrine, and cortisol as before. Shortly after, not only are they singing willingly before peers, they are also taking the stage and performing before large audiences, fully enjoying the moment and experiencing it each time without fear.

They got past it by going through it.

Exposure and habituation are a path forward to face your fears. This is why the only way past your fear is through it. The goal is to expose yourself to the thing that intimidates you and to do it repeatedly until being afraid of it becomes boring to you. When I say fears, I'm talking about fear as it relates to taking risks, launching out, and trying new things as we *HushAndDo*: The fear of failing when you start that business; the fear of the masses not liking your product design; the fear of listeners not enjoying your music; the fear of readers not interested in reading your book! These are the fears I'm focusing on. Now, if you're afraid of spiders and hornets . . . then I'm right there with you. You will not expose me to spiders and wasps and hope there are no negative consequences. You can forget that. Spiders bite and bees sting! I'll conquer that fear in another lifetime.

I urge you to face those fears and not be paralyzed by them because by avoiding them, you never give your nervous system the opportunity to habituate. You never give it the chance to become old and boring, and as a result, the stimulus of those fears remains new with each confrontation. Remember, it's the novel/new thing that is what gets certain hormones released, and our energy and attention increases; it's not the old repeated ones. Dodging your fear will only maintain and magnify it. That's counterproductive and maladaptive to your life. I hate to disappoint you, but, yes, you will fail at times, and things won't go as well as you hoped they would. Do not let that be the grounds for future avoidance. Your skills and abilities to master whatever you're doing grow each time you confront your fear. Think back to the time when you faced fear and overcame it. Remember the sense of pride and accomplishment you had for finally doing it? That feeling is far greater than the feeling of regret and defeat for not trying it at all. You miss 100 percent of the shots you don't take.

To conclude this portion of the conversation, consider the popular Cherokee parable:

A grandfather is talking with his grandson, and he says there are two wolves inside of us that are always at battle. One is a good wolf, which represents things like kindness, bravery, and love. The other is a bad wolf, which represents things like greed, hatred, and fear. The grandson stops and thinks about it for a second, and then he looks up at his grandfather and says, "Grandfather, which one wins?"

The grandfather quietly replies, "The one you feed."

Similarly, I ask you, between flight and avoidance or fight and exposure, which one wins in your life? You must feed fight and exposure regarding your apprehensions. You can't go above them. You can't get around them. You can't get under them. The only way to get to your best days and better tomorrows is to *simply walk through the door of fear*.

Fortunately, you are not the only one dealing with fear, and you won't be the only one walking forward. This entire book serves as an empowering tool to help you take the necessary steps forward.

It's okay to be afraid, but let's put one foot in front of the other as we come to grips with our fears—mine the deep resolve to kick those doors down and enter in. I implore you to abandon the boat of your comfort, dare you to advance even through the midst of treacherous winds and rain, and ask you to answer the call of destiny as He summons you from the waters. We now turn to a powerful biblical story of fear, failure, and faith to encourage and empower us for the rest of our journey.

3.4 Oh, Peter! Don't Be Afraid!

I think Peter often gets a bad rap. He's viewed with a lot of scrutiny. We know he had a mouth on him, displayed violent behavior, at least once, and was unafraid to try his hand in big moments. Peter has many famous stories, but one, in particular, speaks volumes and teaches us a lot about risk, faith, and fear—Peter and Jesus walking on the Galilean waters.

We must review the important context leading up to this miraculous event so we can better appreciate its content, beginning with the parable of the sower with which we dealt earlier (Matthew 13:1–9). There was a sower who went out to sow seeds. Some fell on the roadside where birds came and ate them up. Other seeds were dropped in rocky places where there wasn't much soil. The seeds shot up and grew quickly because there was no depth of soil, but when the sun came out, they were scorched and withered away. Still, some seeds had fallen among the thorns, and the thorns came up and choked them out. Finally, some seeds fell on good soil, and it yielded an amazing return of crops. Confused by Jesus' persistent parable preaching, the disciples asked for an explanation (Matthew 13:18–23). The one explanation I want to put a pin in is the one concerning seed on rocky ground.

"The one on whom seed was sown on the rocky places, this is the man who hears the word, immediately receives it with joy; yet he has no *firm* root in himself, but is *only* temporary, and when affliction or persecution arises because of the word, immediately he falls away" Matthew 13:20–21 (NASB).

The sprout quickly shot out of the rocky ground because the soil was shallow; therefore, it could not afford to grow deep, long-lasting roots. Similarly, the man/woman who isn't deeply rooted in God and His Word can easily be scorched by the sun of persecution and affliction. It's so important to be rooted. Please remember this portion of the story, for I'll recall it momentarily.

After teaching and explaining the parables all throughout Chapter 13, Jesus revisits His hometown of Nazareth to teach in the synagogues. Unfortunately, His hometown hardly believes the man their beloved Jesus has become, and they take offense at His teaching, ultimately, discrediting and rejecting Him. "Is not this the carpenter's son? Is not His mother called Mary, and His brothers, James and Joseph and Simon and Judas?" Matthew 13:55 (NASB). They remembered not only His brothers but His sisters as well, leading them to, ultimately, questioned how He gained so much wisdom and authority. The people's unbelief kept Jesus from doing many miracles there. His hometown rejected him. Adding to the emotional turmoil Jesus was experiencing, Matthew 14 opens with the beheading of His first cousin, John the Baptist. Jesus heard about this and, like any human being, needed a moment to get away to grieve the devastating news about His family. The people heard of this yet still followed him. He had compassion for them and healed the sick among them. Mind you, He's still freshly grieving the murder of His cousin, John. Unable to find a moment to Himself amid the thick crowds remaining, Jesus instructs the disciples to feed them and not send them home. He multiplied two fish and five loaves of bread to feed five thousand people. Immediately after this, He sent the disciples ahead of Him to the other side of the sea, and He sent the crowds away as well. At last, Jesus could have a moment alone to mourn His cousin's tragic death. He went up to the mountain to pray, but the disciples' boat was now far from land and was being battered by heavy winds and waves.

Doesn't this sound just like how life can be sometimes? His heart was bleeding and broken, yet life kept going on despite His feelings. If only He could have had just a day or two to not have to work, be bothered by the needs of people, and just be a normal human being and experience the everyday emotions of grief. . . .

The people knew He was anguished, yet they wouldn't give Him a break. The audience remained. How many of us, like Jesus, still had to come from behind the curtain and greet our audience even though we were suffering on the inside: broken, desperately wishing someone would take the time to recognize our pain and decide for once to meet our needs, instead of waiting for us to meet theirs? Often with tears running down our eyes, it's still *show time*, as our children still need us; as we still have classes to teach; as we still have work deadlines looming. And as much as we yearn for time to stand still, so we can collect ourselves, life simply keeps doing what it always has done—continues to move forward. I want you to put yourself in Jesus' shoes and feel the intensity of these moments in His life. I believe He certainly understands how it feels to be overwhelmed emotionally and to feel like there is no relief in sight. He identifies with those feelings and is present with us through them when life is seemingly overpowering. It's under this emotional duress that Jesus goes to meet His terrified disciples.

Jesus walked on the water to the boat where the disciples were during the fourth watch of the night. This was roughly between the hours of 3 a.m. and 6 a.m. When they saw Him, they thought He was a ghost, and they cried out in fear. In response, Jesus uttered some of His most famous words, which serve as the backdrop for this chapter,

"Take courage, it is I; do not be afraid" Matthew 14:27 (NASB). Consider the next five verses:

28 Peter said to Him, "Lord if it is You, command me to come to You on the water."

29 And He said, "Come!" And Peter got out of the boat, and walked on the water and came toward Jesus.

30 But seeing the wind, he became frightened, and beginning to sink, he cried out, "Lord, save me!"

31 Immediately Jesus stretched out [H]is hand and took hold of him, and said to him, "You of little faith, why did you doubt?"

32 When they got into the boat, the wind stopped.

33 And those who were in the boat worshipped Him, saying, "You are certainly God's Son!

3.5 A Defense for Peter

Many of us have heard this passage preached in church at some point. I have an immediate issue with some of the popular points of this story. Does the text say Peter sank because he took his eyes off Jesus? This is what we always hear, but I don't see that at all in this text. Where in this text did Jesus command Peter to keep his eyes squarely focused on Him and promise he wouldn't drown as a result? It's simply not there, yet these teachings have been popularly imposed on this text. For this reason, I'm here to defend Peter. I'm really here to defend you as well if you've been harshly graded like him.

People really give Peter a hard time because he didn't have a laser-like focus on the face of Jesus during a heavy rain and windstorm in the middle of a lake, as if they wouldn't have even flinched under such adverse conditions. Yeah right! Aren't all the disciples on the boat? Yet, Peter is the only one that dared to get out of the boat and walk to Jesus. He's the only one brave enough to call out to what they thought was a ghost! The rest cried out in fear but Peter cried out in faith.

Being faithfully obedient to Jesus' response, "Come," Peter sets Triple A in motion: Answer, Abandon, and Advance. ***Peter didn't answer Jesus' risky invitation with his mouth but with his feet.*** Full of faith, facing a certain fear of sinking and drowning, Peter decided to *abandon* those in the boat as he began to walk on the water. Verse 29 tells us that Peter got out of the boat, walked on the water, and came toward Jesus. Too often, we imagine this story as Peter getting out of the boat and merely standing in the water, knees knocking and body quivering in trepidation. He finally takes his eyes off Jesus, and that's when he begins to sink. Wrong! Remarkably, to his credit, Peter doesn't just answer Jesus' bid, he *abandons* the fearful ones who remained in the boat and advances toward Jesus. I believe that man deserves a little more recognition than we give him!

Peter's name translated from Greek literally means rock. Imagine the irony of somebody named *Rock*, who is daring to step out into the water to walk to Jesus. Ax heads may float (2 Kings 6.6), certainly the exception to the norm, but typically I haven't found solid rocks to be buoyant. That's almost impossible (depending on the density of said rock). I know that with God all things are possible, and that it's easy to mystify biblical narratives, but let's remember that walking on water is another exception to the norm. It completely defies the laws of physics. That's the second impossibility I see here in this text. However, there's a third impossibility that became quite a reality with Peter. Verse 30 states, "But seeing the wind, he became frightened, and beginning to sink, he cried out, 'Lord, save me!' "

Lightning I have seen before. Rain I have seen before. I have also seen great crashing waves. I have heard thunder on many occasions, but I have never seen wind in my life. I have seen dust and the debris carried by wind, but I have never literally seen wind. While we focus on Peter trying to do the impossible (walk on water), I'm tripping over the fact that Peter is seeing the impossible—the wind! Again, we tend to see this story through the lens of Peter's failure, another Peter mess that Jesus has to straighten out, but I couldn't disagree more. I don't know if Peter had the ability to see wind before this event or not. Maybe he had this gift his entire life, and it's what made him special. I can only speculate. Looking at the immediate text, I see that Peter couldn't see the impossible until he launched out on faith to attempt to do the impossible. There is a phrase I coined, *video ergo est*, meaning ***I see it; therefore, it exists***. If you can imagine it, dream it, and see it, then it's definitely a reality and a possibility for you to achieve. Peter saw the impossible.

As much as I'm lauding Peter, again, I cannot pretend this story did not have its complications. Upon seeing the impossible wind, Peter became frightened and *began* to sink and cried out to Jesus to save him. Immediately, Jesus stretched out His hand and took hold of Peter and saved him, saying, "You of little faith, why did you doubt?" Most times when I've heard this story, it involves wording that connotes imagery of near-death drowning. It's as if Peter was left struggling, panicking, flailing his arms helplessly as he sank to the bottom of the lake, and with his last breath escaping his lungs, he hollered out for Jesus to save him. Just before he loses the last ounce of air keeping him alive, Jesus finally intervenes and rescues Peter mere seconds before his doom with an impatient and condescending tone, "All you had to do was have faith, you idiot!" That couldn't be further from the truth. The text says Peter *began* to sink. It didn't say he sank or was completely submerged or even that he was holding on for dear life. It simply says he began to sink. It's comforting to know that as soon as he began to sink, Jesus extended His hand to save him. He didn't just stand there idly and watch Peter's demise. How cruel and unloving would that have been? It's almost like we're equating Jesus to be the proverbial martial arts sensei from the movies, who uses unconventionally extreme methods to train his student. Is that really how Jesus is? I don't think so.

3.6 How We Are Like Peter

My cousin, Charity, gave me a unique and powerful command years ago that has forever remained with me, "Always take purpose from every situation. No matter what life gives you, always take purpose from it." Before I even begin to settle on whether Peter succeeded or failed, I believe it's first important to extract purpose and a valuable lesson from this episode.

I'm sure Peter would have loved to walk the entire distance from the boat to Jesus on the Sea of Galilee, but he didn't quite make it. He took some steps toward Jesus but began to sink. Recollect the parable of the sower. It is part of a larger context that helps us learn about this water-walking event. Consider the seeds that fell upon the rocky ground. They shot up quickly, but when affliction and tragedy struck, they quickly fell away because they lacked depth. Peter was the only one with the fortitude to respond to what could have possibly been a ghost on the water—Jesus, and he was the only one with the unmitigated gall to dare step onto the water to walk to him. Just like the man who heard the word of the kingdom, but was only established temporarily, perhaps this story reveals that Peter wasn't as deep as he thought he was. Maybe he thought highly of himself as a disciple and saw himself different from the rest who remained safely in the boat. If that's true, because we can only speculate, then, of course, it made sense for him to jump up and take the lead. As he began to sink, we promptly discover he just might not have been as ready as he thought after a few steps on the impossible. Perfection is unattainable in this world, and as a result, failure can and will happen. I urge you not to see failure as the end of the line but as a point of departure. Failure reveals our character. It's a mirror that bears the reflection of our character when things don't go our way. It's easy to be consistent, diligent, energetic, and passionate when things are going well, but what about when things don't go as well? In life, things may not always work your way, but, ultimately, they always work out in your favor.

As we continue to siphon purpose from this, let's consider what we could all agree was a success.

Peter took literal steps on the water and made some progress toward Jesus. Let's applaud that. "But he didn't make it all the way to Jesus!" I choose to look at the glass half full instead. He did do the impossible. That tells me that, to some degree, the impossible is actually quite possible. Perhaps what broke the barrier of the impossible for him was his willingness to try. It certainly opened possibility for Peter. He got off the boat, walked on the water, and came toward Jesus. While on the water attempting one impossible feat, he actually does another impossible feat—he saw the wind! Who do you know that sees wind? I see his walking on water as a success, his beginning to sink as a failure, but his seeing the impossible is another success. It's ironic that he didn't see the wind until after he got out of the boat. Perhaps it's outside the comfort zone of the boat where vision actually becomes clearer, and we're able to see better from a big-picture perspective. Peter and the disciples were terrified when they saw the figure walking on water toward them. They all hollered in fear. He could have empowered his fear by avoiding it, remaining safely in the vessel, or he could have ventured to face his terror and try! You have the same choice to remain or engage as well. The water seems unnerving, but I guarantee that the more we engage in stepping on the water, the less frightening it will become. This is a practical application of the aforementioned mechanism of habituation. There is so much more to experience in the vast ocean of possibility (walking through the door of our fear to get there), than there is to experience in the safe mundane confines of the boat. Finally, look at it from a practical aspect too: will you literally die or be in any physical danger if you try whatever you've been holding back from? There was no physical threat to my existence or the well-being of my family as a result of sitting on that organ bench behind Dr. Vernon. It wasn't going to kill me. Again, that's the lie that fear will try to sell you when braving it. Experiencing it does not escalate it or increase its threat. *Trying* will not kill you. Even if you do fail, you'll be saved!

Peter cried, "Lord, save me!" and *immediately* Jesus stretched out His hand and took hold of him. As soon as Peter began to sink, just as immediately, Jesus extended His hand. The Father will not let you die and watch you drown. Those with small children playing near an outdoor pool can recall the panic that instantaneously seizes you when considering the possibility that they will fall into that pool. Your response to that certainly wasn't delayed, but it was instant. We must allow our thinking to be transformed, and it is here where our worldview of God must begin to be transformed as well. He is not a sadist who takes pleasure in our misfortune. He is a loving father who wants the best for you. Ask yourself, "Why would God, my loving heavenly Father, bid me to step out on the water only to watch me drown and let me suffer?" Is this really what He does? Of course, He will rescue you if you begin to sink.

I believe that's why Jesus said to him, "You of little faith, why did you doubt?" I don't believe it was because Peter unsuccessfully walked all the way to Jesus on the water. I think He was impressed to see an ordinary non-divine human do something extraordinary. Rather, the "you of little faith" part I propose corresponds to Peter's confidence that Jesus would save him! I can imagine Jesus thinking, "Now why would I NOT save you? You really think I'd just stand here and let you drown? I didn't leave the five thousand hungry. I didn't leave the sick unhealed. I didn't leave the demon-possessed bound. I didn't even leave parables unexplained, so why would I leave you?" It's not like Jesus would not do anything unless Peter cried out. He knew the risk of stepping out just as well as Peter did and was ready to intervene no matter how things turned out.

3.7 You Might Sink, But He Will Save

Peter started to sink, and, simultaneously, Jesus started to save him. Peter may not have been fully ready to traverse the waters the whole way, but Jesus is always ready to save. He began to sink, but Jesus saved him. You may have begun to sink in your endeavors, but He's right there ready to save you. He's ready for you to walk all the way to Him and to catch you if you fall—when you fall. You may have begun to give up, but He's picking you up right now. You may have begun to abandon the course of purpose to have an easier life, but He's recalculating right now. You have let your fear of failure and the fear of the "what ifs" hold you hostage and keep you from entering through their necessary doors, but He's giving you the strength right now to say, "no more" and "I will." It's worth noting that the weather didn't change once Peter stepped onto the water, and it didn't change right after he was saved. The storm and the winds did not cease until they got back on the boat. In other words, he faced his trepidation, stepped out the schooner, walked on the water, began to sink, and was immediately rescued, and then the gale ceased. It is quite possible that whatever storms are raging in your heart and mind will keep raging until you finally step out and step forward. Whatever happens will happen, be it failure, success, or a combination of both. You can no longer afford to be paralyzed—seized by the despair of what *could* happen—no more avoidance and door dodging.

Remember, your fear isn't the goon guarding the door to your destiny. Fear is the door, and the only way past it is *through.*

Chapter 4

From Here To Harlem

Either you can embrace deep change or you will be forced to embrace slow death—Robert E. Quinn[17]

In your path to becoming all you are designed to be, change will be a necessary accompaniment throughout the entire process. Sustained greatness requires change. Many would quickly claim they don't mind change or even that they enjoy change, but I've found that everyone can accept change until it's required of them.

We agree with change until it's time for us to participate in changing as well. It's all fun and games until it pushes us out of our comfort zones and introduces new norms. The world is ever changing. Times and people change; therefore, in order for you, and your business, organization, or aspirations, to survive the constant tides of change, you must make a vital decision for the future: deep change or slow death. Slow death begins when someone, confronting the dilemma of making deep organizational changes or accepting the status quo, rejects the option for deep change.[18] Previous chapters dealt with some deep issues of the heart and soul. In a similar nature, we must continue on the deep inward journey. Whatever work that change needs to make in our lives, it cannot be a superficial one. It must run deep and address core beliefs in our hearts and minds. How can you better surrender to change?

Let's be clear about something while we trek toward becoming our best selves. There's a difference between incremental change and deep change. The former has a desired goal in mind and can be obtained after careful analysis and planning. It comes with steps that are precisely followed to complete the goal. For all intents and purposes, this is practical advice for *HushAndDo*, but I want us to go deeper than that. Deep change involves a paradigm shift. It demands and embraces new behaviors, new perspectives, surrendering control, and taking risks. Often times, individuals and organizations will avoid the pain and struggle that accompanies deep change, yet by doing so, they have also chosen slow death. It's the difference between Walmart and F. W. Woolworth's.

4.1 Deep Change versus Incremental Change

Deep change is the best way to confront slow death; although, it is not the easiest. Personal change involves taking the inward expedition into the land of the unknown, which is a place of new thinking, new patterns, risk-taking, and confronting issues. At some point, you have to ask yourself some real questions: Am I achieving what I desire? Is what I'm doing getting me there? How has the way I've currently done things worked so far? Here, one must also break the logic of task pursuit, which is to be so focused on completing tasks that the right things are not being done. It's an obsession with being busy. Personal change involves seeing the bigger picture, which is more than just completing tasks. It is obtaining a new and fresh perspective and putting reason and purpose behind all that we do. It demands integrity, and it is organic. It is a bridge that is being built as one walks on it. It is not contrived from a linear equation or formula but is created from the demand of the current need for change and transformation. To make incremental change is not enough, as usually those changes are mere extensions of the past. Yes, the carpet may be new and gives a fresh look to your room, but your thinking remains to be stale. Great, you went out and got a new logo for your business, but you're still handling business the same way you always did. In pursuing deep change, we need to redesign our road maps and realign ourselves with our surrounding environment. We reinvent ourselves by changing our perspective.[19] We endeavor to remain relevant in what we do.

We have all heard the saying, "If it's not broken, then don't fix it." However, such a statement comes from an incremental change worldview. In a church context, for example, incremental changes can be things like the location of the instruments, the genre of music for worship, or how long a worship service lasts. I'm not suggesting that everyone should spontaneously turn the tables upside down and shake things up just to be different. I am calling for deep change and personal transformation because this will position us for long life instead of slow death. As a man, a husband, and father, this causes me to evaluate areas in my life and ministry that are perhaps inconsistent. Before I concentrate on anything external, this is a call for internal transformation to become more like Christ. This is a call for the development of integrity and character. Perhaps there's a way you've been taught your whole life or a method that's been exampled for you. Again, one of the principles of *HushAndDo* is transformational thinking, which leads to transformational living. The kind of change you and I need requires that we abandon the past, but not our history.

I want to be gentle in my approach here as I lay out the difference between the past and history. Words like change, new, and fresh usually engender some level of anxiety in people, especially if they are of a seasoned age. We casually throw around clichés like "out with the old and in with the new." Let me carefully address a potential pitfall in this. All cultures across the world have core principles and ideals upon which their community stands, otherwise known as cultural values. For example, *future orientation* is a western cultural value. Here in the United States, we are obsessed with having the latest and newest "everything," whether it be a cell phone, a television, fashion trends, you name it. And newness sells. On the contrary, the farther east you travel, you will discover that eastern cultures maintain a cultural value of *past orientation.* This cultural value is rooted in the past and existing events, traditions, and norms. Products are marketed with sayings like "It worked for your grandparents. It worked for your parents. You can be assured it will work for you too." It concerns itself with how future change can fit with the past. Now you're probably wrestling with what appears to be a conflict regarding *future and past orientations*, as I indicated that incremental change usually is just extensions from the past. No particular cultural value is superior to another. There may be differences in each that work especially well at certain times, but one is not inherently better. To suggest that would also imply that certain cultures are better than others. However, I've stressed that part of deep change requires a series of new: new thinking, new paradigms, and new behaviors. Yes, we must abandon the past, but we must never forget history. The past you leave behind, but history you carry with you into the future. The past focuses on what was done and how it was done. History focuses on who did it and why they did it. Of course, as times goes on, new methodologies are necessary to stay with the times of this ever-changing world. "Excellence never lies within the boxes drawn in the past."[20] However, we must never forget those who came before us and blazed trails so we could be where we are now. History is our bridge and our corrective from which we learn how to better navigate into the future. Change is not exclusively for younger people; it is for everyone. I've found that one of the best ways to keep everyone involved with change is to honor the history of those who've come before us. As you honor them, they will be more inclined to participate in leaving the past behind and march forward into the future by your side. Nobody wants to be forgotten. Abandon the past but keep history.

I am not preaching change for the sake of change, but it is necessary for the sake of *HushAndDo*. How can you as an individual, you as your business, goals, and ideas, move forward to a successful future unless you take the time to take personal inventory and consider where you can change and be transformed? This exercise will position you for so much more than just accomplishment, goal obtainment, or success. As you transform your thinking, your living will be transformed as well. There comes a time where you have to ask yourself some difficult questions. Am I accomplishing what I desire to accomplish? Am I arriving at my goals? Am I making progress? Is what I'm doing right now to get there yielding success? Is it working? Is it time to change things up, including myself? In one way or another, whether voluntarily or involuntarily, you have changed many times during your life. You look back, and say to yourself, "I had to change."[21]

4.2 Realizing the Need for Change

I was privileged to participate in a joint communications-workshop where the aim was to help my colleagues and me to better understand each other as it related to our approaches to creativity, communication, and change. To begin the day, the first exercise required that we all stand in a circle around a standing loop circle on the floor. First, we were supposed to change positions with our partner in the circle, and second, we had to pass through the loop on the floor. The facilitator grabbed her stopwatch and waited for our mark, set, and ready—go, to time us. For the first trial, we each took turns walking through the circle and switched positions with our partner opposite the circle. Each pair went one by one until all had changed positions with their respective partner and had passed through the circle on the floor. This took us about fifteen seconds. Encouraged by the facilitator to get it done faster, we did the same thing for the second trial and got our time down to thirteen seconds. After the third trial, time was down to ten seconds. We were ready for the fourth trial, and by this time we had formed a highly efficient plan of attack on how to accomplish the task at hand. Nobody bumped into each other, and the exchange of position was effortless and quick. A few more trials ensued, and we yielded similar results. Finally, the facilitator stopped us and informed us that most groups doing this exercise could get it done in under one second. One second! The thought of completing that challenge in under one second seemed impossible, yet she assured us it could be done. Before continuing the same routine, we concluded that the way we had been approaching the task simply wouldn't get the job done. We needed to stop and think about new and creative ways of approach. We asked each other and the facilitator questions about the rules of the game and sought clarification on what we could and could not do. After a brief moment of thinking and strategizing, we initiated another trial, and our time decreased exponentially! We were down to about two seconds now. We thought some more, fine-tuned our approach, and by the third trial in our new system, we were well under one second. We realized the need for change. One way was efficient, but after a while, it no longer served a purpose. We had to change. You're probably wondering what did we do to figure it out, aren't you? I won't tell you. Get a group together, and try it yourselves, and see if you can beat our amazing time of six-hundredths of a second. Good luck!

Few people are good at reinventing themselves. They often choose the destructive alternative of staying busy. It may not be effective behavior, but it has the effect of a good narcotic. It diverts attention from the real issue and temporarily saves them from having to tackle and resolve the actual problems.[22] The real issue was that it was time to change. Otherwise, we could never have completed the challenge in record time.

How long will you keep doing things the way you always have and keep thinking the way you've always thought before you change? You can cling to the old ways as tight as you'd like, but as you do, your dreams, aspirations, and goals will begin to experience a slow death. If you own a record store, you can't exclusively sell 8-tracks and cassette tapes and expect to stay open for long. We all know the principal platform for listening to music now is digital: MP3s, WAVs, Pandora, Spotify, etc. You can still be a record store, but unless you find a way to be relevant for today, your store will continually become more and more irrelevant. How many of us are still applying 8-track and cassette tape methodologies to 21st-century life? Music will always be relevant, but our method of hearing it will change with the times. I challenge you to take a critical look at what you're doing and recognize its permanent principles and distinguish that from the temporal methods to accomplish it. God Himself proclaimed in Malachi 3:6, "For I, the Lord, do not change." Hebrews 13:8 even says, "Jesus Christ is the same yesterday and today and forever" (NASB). This is true of God, yes. He does not change in principle or in who He is. He is immutable, but please know, that while He Himself does not change, His methodologies certainly do. How will you respond when God changes the methodology? Let's take a Jericho stroll to an ancient Middle-Eastern story that further gives us insight on change.

4.3 Joshua Fit the Battle of Jericho

You may talk about then men of Gideon. You may talk about the men of Saul. But there's none like the good old Joshua at the battle of Jericho. This story is popular within the church and has permeated popular culture as well. The Israelites' conquest into the Promised Land, Canaan (which corresponds to modern-day Israel, Jordan, Lebanon, and Syria), began with the battle of Jericho. God commanded Joshua to have all the warriors and seven priests bearing the ark of the covenant to walk around Jericho once a day for six consecutive days. The only people to make any noise or sound were the priests blowing the seven ram's horns. The people were instructed to remain quiet until the command was given to shout. On the seventh day, they were to march around Jericho seven times in the same manner as the previous six days. However, on the seventh lap, the people were to shout. They did just as they were instructed, and once they shouted on day seven, the mighty walls of Jericho came tumbling down. I'm sure you're wondering what this has to do with Harlem (the title of this chapter), change, and *HushAndDo*. Keep reading.

If you've been to church before, this story has been taught for years. In many instances, it has been re-enacted in live church services. The preacher would instruct the congregation to stand up and walk around the sanctuary seven times and to shout on the seventh lap, reenacting Joshua and Jericho. It's one of the more popular stories of the Old Testament. To put things in a more realistic context, I thought about Jericho and juxtaposed it to a modern-day city. I'm sure Jericho was not the size of an auditorium or sanctuary: 100-seat, 500-seat, 5000-seat, etc., auditorium. Jericho was an entire city! Scholars are not sure of the actual size of biblical Jericho, but without a doubt, the city of Jericho was around for many years, even during the Bronze Age, long before the Hebrew conquest. Therefore, let's imagine this incredible feat in present-day.

For the sake of the illustration, let's use Cleveland, Ohio, for a modern-day Jericho. I want us to wrap our minds around the fact that Joshua marched around an entire city and not a small room that represented an entire city. What would it take to walk around Cleveland thirteen times? I won't bore you with the math, but I made several calculations. Based on approximation and rounding to the nearest whole number, to walk around Cleveland thirteen times (1x per day for six days + 7x in one day, just as Joshua and the Israelites did) would roughly be 468 miles on foot!

It is roughly 468 miles from here to Harlem, New York!

By this point in Israel's history, God had done a lot for them. He sent the plagues in Egypt to initiate the Exodus. He sent the pillar of cloud to lead them by day and the pillar of fire to guide them by night. He parted the Red Sea so they could cross over on dry land. He caused water to emerge from a rock while they were in the desert. When they were hungry, He caused bread to fall from heaven. God even caused them to be victorious in one battle, so long as Moses kept his hands lifted. They even crossed the Jordan River on dry land to get to this point before Jericho, and that location of the Jordan River isn't even that deep! Much of the emphasis until now is on the great deeds God did on behalf of His people. No doubt, they would have realized the significant meaning of the number seven and observed its repetition in their instructions. God created the world in six days, but on the seventh, He rested and made it a Sabbath. Seven is known as the number of perfection and the number of creation. Seven is equated with rest. The number seven and rest/Sabbath even impacted agriculture. For six years, the Israelites could work their fields. However, in the seventh year, there was to be absolutely no pruning or sowing seed in the land. They could eat of the land, but God commanded the land to have complete Sabbath rest.

For six days, once a day, they marched. Seven priests led the way each day blowing seven ram's horns, and on the seventh day, they walked around seven times. The reoccurrence of the number seven could possibly have primed Israel's expectations of what would happen here at Jericho—rest! But what happens when God seemingly changes the script? How ironic is it that although God does not change, but He ordains change daily concerning His creation? God is a change agent. I'm sure they expected some form of rest, hush and rest, hence the number seven; however, God commanded quite the opposite—hush and march. On the seventh day of this new creation of Old Testament history, they don't rest. God confounds expectations and has them walk miles upon miles, miles of marching for the sake of fulfilling destiny and arriving at what He promised them. Can you imagine people's faces and your face if this was Cleveland, and we had to log in 468 miles to get to our promise?

Allow me to interject another consideration of distance. Psalm 103:11 (NASB) says, "For as high as the heavens are above the earth, so great is His loving kindness toward those who fear Him." The heavens is a broad term referring to the sky, stars, and planets. In calculating the distance of His steadfast love, I chose our sun as the reference point for the heavens since the entire Milky Way Galaxy and all its bodies revolve around it. The sun is roughly 93 million miles from Earth. Traveling at the speed of light, photons emitted from the sun's surface reach Earth in an average of eight minutes and twenty seconds. I imagined building a highway that stretched from Earth all the way to the surface of the sun. We load up for the road trip of life in this hypothetical example, suspending the issues of gravity, lack of oxygen, extreme freezing temperatures, as we leave the incendiary temperatures of Earth's atmosphere and draw near to the sun. If we were to drive on that imaginary freeway without stops, traveling 65 miles per hour, it would take roughly a little more than 63 years to reach sun! What am I saying? It would take on average more than two lifetimes to drive the distance, which is represented as the height of God's love for us! I could take the rest of this life, the next one, and the one after, driving at 65 miles per hour and only make it to the sun's surface. We haven't even considered venturing into the sun's core. One hundred and sixty-three years only scratches the surface. Feel the enormity of this distance and these numbers. Overwhelming, isn't it? And such is the vast depth and intensity of God's love for us! Contemplating the astronomic distance of His love for me, the distance of His willingness and passion for me, coming from Heaven to Earth to show the way, I reckon that the 468 miles from here to Harlem isn't that bad.

I challenge myself, first and foremost, and then all of us to consider the following: What is your work ethic? What is the level of your grind, grit, and hustle in achieving all that is attainable for you in this life? What is the degree of your diligence? How deep is your passion? Are you willing to make the necessary changes to get to where you want to get to in life? Are you embracing deep change or slow death? You must be honest with yourself. Denial occurs when we are presented with painful information about ourselves, information that suggests we need to make a deep change, and yet we do nothing about it.[23] We frequently hear the cliché, "Go the extra mile," but in this context, it's both literal and figurative. Are we willing to go the extra mile, to make the extra effort for the sake of achievement and accomplishment? Are we willing to accept change and adapt to new ways God might move and the new challenges life may present us? How many of us would have quickly fatigued after just a few miles? How many of us have an aversion to change and would resist the application of a new methodology? Would you resist the new perspective and still try to force things the way they have always been in the past? How hard are you going to labor and strive for what is yours? Will you settle and give up? Or, will you quiet yourself, lace up your walking shoes, and get to moving—

careful to obey the instructions given to you for seeing miracles accomplished before your very eyes? I simultaneously consider how much more difficult it would have been to knock down Jericho's walls (in Bible times) in my own strength using hammers or anything I could find. Again, I consider that a Jericho stroll from here to Harlem isn't that bad. I'm going to fight, climb, sweat, and toil for what's mine!

4.4 Will You Change?

Pastor Gwen McCurry always says, "You have just about enough of Jesus as you want!" She realized that Christ did not force Himself on people, but the depth of one's personal relationship with Him is entirely up to each individual. God's end is clear. He wants to have a deep, loving relationship with us and is ready. It is up to us to decide how much we want to let Him into our hearts. The spiritual implications here are replete, but this can be applied to so much more. You have just about as much success in life as you want. To position yourself for greatness and to accomplish all that's in your destiny, you must make the internal commitment to change, to contend, and to be consistent. Empower yourself. Will yourself to win! We cannot wait on pastors, bosses, or celebrities to affirm and empower us to do what we know is right. The impetus must come from within.

Will you accept the seeming change? I say seeming because when you think about it, all the Israelites had to do was march, and all they had been doing until this point was marching! God commenced the Exodus, and they marched. He sent the cloud and the sun, and they marched. He parted the Red Sea, and they marched. They drank from the water of the rock, and then they marched. The Red Sea was split open to dry land, and they marched.

It's the same hustle, the same grind, the same passion, the same faith and perseverance you've always had, but now it's time to apply a new methodology to see the new that's coming your way! Remember history but abandon the past. What are the different steps I can take to accomplish my goals, my dreams, and to walk in purpose? How can I realign myself to my core values and be true to what I've been gifted to do? Perhaps you've gotten off track and have begun pursuing the wrong ends, like chasing money instead of chasing purpose, for example. That's where loss of alignment occurs. I've been believing. I'll still believe. I've had faith. I'm still having faith. They are the same principles and statues but applied differently as our world continues to change. The difference is now that faith, that belief, that drive, and that passion demand that I work a little harder this time and strive just a little more and be open to change.

And to see the miraculousness in my life,

And to see walls come down in my life,

And to see complete victory in my life,

I'll continue to march on—even if it's from here to Harlem.

Chapter 5

The Abundance Of Rain

The story of the prophet Elijah and the great demonstration on Mount Carmel, found in 1 Kings 18, is popular in Judaism and Christianity. It came down to a public display of divine response and power to prove to Israel that there, indeed, was no other God but Jehovah. This passage culminates in a large gathering of the entire nation, waiting to see if the god of the prophets of Baal would respond by fire or if Elijah's God would. He organizes a competition between the two gods and their prophets—Elijah against the world, 850 prophets of Baal and Asherah versus just one lone prophet of

Yahweh.[e] They both were given a bull for the sacrifice. The God who responded by fire would be crowned the winner. The prophets of Baal tarried and self-mutilated to get their gods to answer them, but to no avail. Along came Elijah's turn, and God responded with fire, proving Himself real for all to see. This is a tremendous story that catapulted Elijah into the history books as one of Israel's most prolific prophets. The context of this story reveals the importance of our call to *HushAndDo* and the responsibility we have to each other and to our communities. It will all tie together once we glance behind the scenes.

5.1 Setting the Stage for a Great Display

We are introduced to the prophet Elijah, at the beginning of 1 Kings 17, with a bit of his biography and the region's meteorology, from which we can

---

[e] It is worth noting that Elijah was indeed not the only prophet of Yahweh, for as Queen Jezebel was killing off the prophets of Yahweh, Obadiah hid 100 of them in a cave.

begin to understand the region's economy as well. Four key verses will anchor the context, and I'll juxtapose them with Elijah's great demonstration on the mountain: 1 Kings 17:1, 17:7, 18:1, and 18:2. "As the LORD, the God of Israel lives, before whom I stand, surely there shall be neither dew nor rain these years, except by my word" 17:1b, (NASB).

In biblical times, both the Old Testament and New Testament were agrarian societies. There weren't major big businesses competing or high consumerism or advanced industrial goods or advanced technology. All they had, primarily, was land, produce, and livestock, and these drove the economy. Years of no rain in a Middle-Eastern-desert country would have severely impacted the entire region. Although Elijah was Yahweh's prophet, even he was not exempt from suffering these adverse climate conditions. God sent him east of the Jordan River to reside during this severe drought. There he drank from the wadi,[f] and

---

[f] A wadi is mostly found in Northern African and the Middle East. It is a small watercourse that only has water during periods of rain.

ravens brought him bread and meat. Unfortunately, the stream dried up because there was no rain in the land (17:7). Then, he was sent to Zarephath where the Lord had prearranged more food and drink for him.

It's easy to lose touch with Elijah's reality because the text advances the story quickly. During this famine, he has now relocated twice! I'm sure you are aware of the hassle it takes to relocate and move. From what we can see in the text, his move had nothing to do with a new job or his desire for new scenery or, like many of us—depending on where we live (especially us Northerners)—to even escape the climate. His relocating had everything to do with his basic needs, namely food and water. He moved to wherever he could find nourishment or wherever there were provisions for food and water. Once he arrived at his new town, he met a widow who had exactly what he needed. Ironically, she had just enough meal and oil to make one last serving for her and her son, but instead, she prepared some food for Elijah. Because of her generosity, she experienced a miraculous unending supply of oil and meal to help her family endure the famine. Please remember that it still had not rained—the famine was setting in and beginning to worsen.

"After many days the word of the Lord came to Elijah, in the third year [of the drought], saying, 'Go, show yourself to Ahab, and I will send rain upon the earth'" (1Kings 18:1, ESV[g]). Three years of drought have now taken place, and there was still no rain. By this time, the famine's impact on their economy was devastating indeed. "So, Elijah went to present himself to Ahab. The famine was severe in Samaria" (18:2). The prophet obediently met with King Ahab. Upon seeing him, he addressed Elijah as the "troubler of Israel." Allow me a deliberate digression here. Rest assured that whenever you're doing something great—trailblazing, altering life, or history changing—someone will view you as the antagonist and falsely label you. If you're not a troubler, then you're a liar; if not a liar, then an opportunist; if not an opportunist, then a loser. During the peak of the Civil Rights Movement, plenty of people, pastors, and ministers disagreed with Dr. Martin Luther King Jr.'s approach to social justice and civil rights.

---

[g] English Standard Version

He was known as Martin "Loser" King Jr. in those days. He certainly wasn't the highly celebrated champion we currently revere every year. It's also true regarding Malcolm X, one of the most maligned prophets of his time. We even see this prevalent with the 44th president of the United States, Barack Obama, and his push for health-care reform. Can you remember how his opponents scrutinized him so heavily? As good as the idea seemed, many vehemently opposed the Affordable Care Act and failed to see the much-needed direction of that legislation in our country, which is affordable health-care for the least of these. I'm sure you can remember the criticisms you've encountered in your life as you sought to pursue your goals and accomplish what you strongly felt was in you to do:

"Who does she think she is?"

"You're so naïve to believe you can change the world!"

"What makes you so special that you can do this or do that?"

"You think you're better than me?"

All these questions, suspicions, and criticisms just because you dared, declared, and shared your aspirations with others. Just imagine the response you'll get when you finally do achieve what you've set out to do! Let these small discouragements now strengthen you for the deeper criticism that is sure to come later. Teach them the 50/50 Rule (Chapter 7), and apply it to yourself, first and foremost, and reach Stevie Wonder's "Higher Ground":

Teachers, keep on teaching.

Preachers, keep on preaching.

Lovers, keep on loving.

Believers, keep on believing.[24]

To this I add . . .

Prophets, keep on prophesying.

Builders, keep on building.

Innovators, keep on innovating.

Creators, keep on creating.

Whatever you're supposed to be doing, whatever you're called to be doing, whatever you're good at doing—focus on that, and keep doing that thing! You may be wondering how long you should keep at it? Mr. Wonder answered that question in the same song: "'Till I reach my highest ground!"

5.2 The Famine Is Still Here

There remained to be a severe drought and famine in Israel and Samaria in 1 Kings 18. In the midst of this three-plus-year dearth, we arrive at the most popular story in Elijah's ministry, the fire demonstration to prove who is real and who the illusion is. We looked at what the prophets of Baal did for their portion of the demonstration and how they miserably failed despite crying and cutting themselves all day. Imagine your local news sports anchor giving a suspenseful play-by-play call of this live event:

As every eye of the nation rests its gaze on him, the prophet Elijah begins to prepare his sacrifice. The perpetual question at hand is, Will his God respond by fire or not? We have nothing for the prophets of Baal. Hopefully, Elijah can show us something. He's motioning for everyone to come near him. The tension out here is palpable! You can cut it with a knife! He is repairing the altar of his God by using twelve stones. He keeps looking up at the sky and motioning as if he's talking directly to his God. They are building trenches around his altar now, fairly wide trenches at that. Now he's arranging the firewood and putting the bull he's cut carefully on top of it. Folks, this is customary. He should be ready to go in a moment.

Now wait! He's motioning toward some helpers. We're listening in live, and I can't believe what I'm hearing! He's asking them to fill four jars of water. I have no idea where Elijah is going with this, but they are filling the jars as we speak. He motions. Ladies and gentlemen, in an unprecedented manner, he is actually pouring the water from the jars on top of the bull and the firewood. He has literally poured all that water over everything! This is madness! I don't know how this thing will catch fire now, but—oh no . . . NO! He did it again! He filled the four jars again. He's pouring water over everything—again! This is unthinkable.

Folks, you won't believe it, but he's doing it a third time, yes, a third time! And that's it. He's poured water on this altar three times over! The bull is soaked. The firewood is soaked. The trenches are filled with water. Elijah the Tishbite is making it darn near impossible for anything on that altar to catch fire now that it's drenched. Perhaps he's throwing the game. Does he want to lose? Surely, by now, all he can do is pray.

Indeed, Elijah then did pray, uttering only a few words:

"O Lord, God of Abraham, Isaac, and Israel, let it be known this day that You are God in Israel and that I am Your servant and have done all these things at Your command. Answer me, O Lord! Answer me, so that this people may know that You, the Lord, are God, and that You have turned their hearts back again" 1 Kings 18:36b-37 (NASB).

Permit me another succinct yet urgent digression, please. If you're going to do something big, and if you're going to gather a big audience to do so, just make sure God told you to do it! How foolish Elijah would have looked, and how fatal it would surely have been for him to have done everything of his own will—not by the unction of God. Please, just do what He's telling you to do!

The fire of the Lord fell and consumed the ox, the firewood, the stones, the dust, and licked up all the water on and around the altar. As a result, the people fell on their faces and confessed, "The Lord indeed is God; the Lord indeed is God." Pouring water out and drenching the altar eliminated any potential speculation about how fire consumed everything. Saturating the altar with H_2O (the chemical formula for water), aborted all potential allegations of "spontaneous combustion" long before they were even conceptualized. The prophets of Baal lost the demonstration. They were then seized and executed. Elijah then said to Ahab, "Go up, eat and drink; for there is the sound of abundance of rain." The drought finally ended, and it began to rain heavily shortly thereafter. The region and its economy could finally recover and rebuild.

5.3 A MAJOR Sacrifice

The three-plus years of drought and famine had come to an end. Let's review the four context verses, key to anchor the discussion: It was declared in 17:1 that there would be no dew or rain except by God's Word. The wadi from which Elijah drank dried up in 17:7 because there was no rain in the land. The lack of rain created hardship for everybody, including the widow of Zarephath and her son, yet she was hospitable to Elijah. By the time he presented himself to King Ahab, the drought had already lasted three years (18:1). We no longer had to speculate or imagine about the conditions of the region because 18:2 finally makes it plain; the famine was severe. Thrust thoroughly into relentless destitution, affecting all people, Elijah took jars filled with water and poured them out as a sacrifice to the Lord, at His behest, and for the people as well. All of this led up to the big point I've been luring you with for this entire chapter. Here's what I can't stop thinking about:

- There was no rain or dew for more than three years.
- FROM WHERE DID ELIJAH GET THE WATER?
- Even more critical than that question itself, which could have hundreds of answers, is the motivation and rationale for what Elijah did.
- WHY DID YOU DO IT, ELIJAH?

Rainfall drives agriculture. After three long, arduous, and famishing years of drought, I can only imagine just how invaluable water was. The famine affected everybody, including God's own prophet, Elijah. It caused him to have to relocate several times, again, just for survival. Imagine the value *any amount of water* would have had at the end of these three frustrating and oppressive years. He wasn't the only person pushed to the brink of survival. It was brutal to all people in the vicinity. Elijah could have sold the water he had for a great monetary gain. He could have ensured his own future by keeping it for himself until the end of the drought. He could have even given his water to the poor, and to people who didn't have access to water, to the marginalized who no doubt suffered catastrophic losses during this famine. We still don't know where Elijah got enough water to pour out twelve times over. Addressing that question is not as paramount to our life of *HushAndDo* as is addressing his motive and the nationwide impact of his offering. He poured out the water before the Lord, as a sacrifice, to help the nation realize that God was real and that they needed Him dearly.

Let's have a quick science class and review the states of matter! We'll combine science with a narrative-critical form of reading a biblical text—focusing directly on the words of the text in a story—to uncover the critical points within a pericope. I earlier mentioned the chemical formula for water is H_2O. It exists in a solid state as ice, in a liquid state as water, and in a gas state as water vapor or steam. When you heat water past its 100 degrees Celsius[h] boiling point, it doesn't simply disappear, but that water turns into steam and evaporates into the atmosphere. Clouds are formed in the sky when the motion of all the various water molecules slows. They begin to turn into water droplets; once the air around them cools, since it was a high temperature that caused them to vaporize, the cooler temperature causes them to return to water. When this happens in the sky, clouds form, and, before long, it begins to pour rain.

Elijah told Ahab to go eat and drink, for he heard the sound of the abundance of rain! Shortly after that, the sky turned dark, and it rained tumultuously! I suggest that the water Elijah poured out to God for the people turned into a vapor that soon condensed and caught wind of cooler air. That then turned into rain—a rain that poured over the entire region, and thus, began a period of recovery and rebuilding. His personal sacrifice of water created an atmosphere (storm

---

[h] 212 degrees Fahrenheit

clouds over the region) that would bless everyone far more than just himself.

What you and I are gifted to do and are purposed to do in this life has a people and a place for which these deeds are meant to impact, help, heal, mend, grow, revitalize, and rebuild. The world is full of problems, and I believe the solutions lie within each of us. What we bring to the table through our gifts and talents—ultimately expressed in unique ways through the matrix of our personalities—is exactly what the world needs. I believe there is a *Jay T-sized* void in this world and that the Creator put the solution to that problem in me. People are waiting for me to manifest and step forth in my destiny so they can be cured, enlightened, healed, loved, helped, consoled, and rescued. There are people waiting for my sacrifice, for my gift, and my offering. ***You have a purpose, and there are a people waiting on you too, who, whether they realize it or not, desperately need you.*** Your willingness to pour out your gifts and talents and lend them for the benefit of mankind determines the level they will be impacted. Elijah didn't keep the water for himself, but he poured it out, and in return, it created rain for thousands of people. You have valuable gifts and ideas inside you that if kept to yourself and not poured out may cause you not to reach as many people as you potentially can. This *HushAndDo* thing is so much bigger than we are in achieving what we want in life and securing happiness and survival for ourselves alone. We are blessed to be a blessing. And because of the greatness inside you, you have a great responsibility to pour it out for others. You are needed! We all have benefited from someone else's sacrifice in our lives, directly and indirectly. We are already indebted to others who have lived a life of service for the betterment of mankind. I believe the way we say thank you for those sacrifices is by continuing the legacy of selflessness in service, prioritizing any opportunity to help make life a little better for someone else. It's in you to do that. It's what Elijah did. That widow gave up her last meal for him to live, probably not realizing at the time that God was positioning him to impact hundreds of people. She could have single-handedly stopped Elijah's process had she kept her water and meal for herself; but instead, she gave it out. She had every right to keep the food and drink for her family, but she didn't. She was an example of altruism in his life. He lived out his "thank you" by pouring out his water on Mount Carmel before thousands.

Perhaps you wrestle with the feeling that what you have to offer is insignificant. Perhaps, like me, you struggle with self-esteem and wonder if what you can offer is even worth anything. I'm here to affirm to you and let you know it most certainly is! The struggle to constantly renounce false beliefs and to re-stand ourselves on truth is ongoing. It's possible that you've tried it before, and you failed, or have experienced some setbacks. If you're honest with yourself, you're afraid to try again. Your past failures and mistakes may intimidate you. For many of us, these two also bully and paralyze us, keeping us from moving forward and trying again. It's okay to be afraid.[i] I give you permission to be afraid because it's a human emotion. I give you permission to be a human being! Even after such a grand demonstration and obvious victory, Elijah still dealt with fear. Queen Jezebel swore Elijah's death, despite his God proving to be real. The wife of Israel's head of state

---

[i] Feel free to read chapter 3 again if you haven't quite conquered fear since then. ☺

wanted him dead. So yes, you have permission to be afraid. But the fear cannot paralyze us and keep us from moving forward in our lives.

There is a greater good and a greater calling we must serve. We may fail. We will fail, but I'm so darn glad He let me try it again![25] It does not matter how big or small your gift may seem; it will always have limits while being kept in your hands, but when you release those gifts and put them in the hands of God, I promise you there are wonders He can do with the seemingly little you have.

Moses just had a rod, yet God used it to split deep seas and produce water from stone. David just had five smooth stones, yet somehow one of those stones was enough in God's hand to defeat an entire army of Philistines and to create a complete career change for Dave, who would later take the highest office in the land as king. The little boy only had two fish and five loaves of bread. He offered it up and poured it out, and shortly afterward, thousands of people were fed. Elijah, fighting for his own survival, just had several jars of water, but he poured them out. He gave them up, and it rained for everyone. Jesus, a child refugee and carpenter's son, born into abject poverty with a bounty on His head, gave not just His gifts and talents, but He gave His very life as a sacrifice, putting Himself in God's care by saying, "Father, into your hands I commend my spirit" Luke 23:46 (NASB). He became the Savior of the world and the Redeemer of all. The Creator has a knack for multiplication and exponential growth, as you can see. You may fall short or fail, but please, for the sake of this world that desperately needs you, don't stop. Keep on striving. Keep on thinking. Keep on creating. Do not stop. You cannot stop. This thing is bigger than you are. You have a responsibility. Won't you put your gifts, your ideas, your creativity, and talents into His hands? Watch what He does with them and how many people can benefit from your commitment to Hushing and Doing and entrusting your life and work to Him.

Nevertheless, we must go deeper. What are your jars of water that will greatly benefit your community? What are your two fish and five loaves? What do you have in your hands, your mind, or your heart that can possibly benefit an entire nation? I cannot answer that question for you, but I can turn on some lights so you can see it better. Greatness awaits.

Chapter 6

God's Got Me!

Everybody in Cleveland, Ohio, can remember the summer of 2016. Most can remember the time and place they were at when our Cleveland Cavaliers won their first NBA championship and ended a 52-year major league sports title drought. Cleveland's beloved son and hero, LeBron James, took home MVP honors for that series, and rightfully so. The way he played was absolutely mesmerizing. Finally winning a championship for his hometown, the discussions quickly resurfaced about who was the greatest basketball player of all time. The discussion has always featured Michael Jordan at the top without much debate. Now, this conversation includes Kobe Bryant, LeBron James, and some enter Kevin Durant into the equation. Fans rally behind their favorite NBA superstars in full confidence that their team will win the championship because of who they have on the team. You've heard, "We got Steph Curry! He's lethal from downtown!" or "We got LeBron James. He is the greatest player on the planet!" or "Nobody can stop James Harden's step-back!" or "We're going to the ship because we got Kyrie!" These are the expressions we frequently hear everywhere. Everybody is confident in their team because they are confident they have the greatest player on their squad. They'll win because of who they got.

How does one define greatness? In a general societal definition, it's all about having bigger, badder, and boast of the most. In the context of sports, it's defined by a player's individual accomplishments, contributions to the league, and, ultimately, championships. In business, it's measured by how much revenue a company profits generate and how influential its brand is. In music, greatness can be defined by recording songs and albums that transcend time and sell over one million units. However, you may not be an athlete, a business owner, or an artist. Do we want to enter the rat race of acquiring goods and fame to prove that we are great? How can the rest of us achieve greatness in our lives?

6.1 A Biblical Definition of Greatness

The discussion of greatness arises in the Bible within the Gospel According to Luke. At His own supper, just hours before His brutal flogging and execution, Jesus presented an alternative interpretation of what it means to be great, much to the shock and dismay of His followers:

> And there arose also a dispute among them as to which one of them was regarded to be the greatest. And He said to them, "The kings of the Gentiles lord it over them; and those who have authority over them are called 'Benefactors.' But it is not this way with you, but the one who is the greatest among you must become like the youngest, and the leader like the servant. For who is greater, the one who reclines at the table or the one who serves? Is it not the one who reclines at the table? But I am among you as the one who serves" Luke 22:24–27 (NASB).

Jesus is speaking to the normal assumptions of grandeur when it comes to greatness. Imagine a dinner where highly esteemed guests, heads of state, and political leaders are invited. You can already think of some of the names of the people who would be sitting at the table. You're in the company of presidents, prime ministers, queens, kings, and celebrities from all over the world. You're feeling privileged to be in the room with them, and you think to yourself, "Oh this is great! I'm in the room with all the greats!" The aroma of exquisitely prepared morsels fills your nose. You see the clamoring chatter of all the guests as they begin to locate their seats at the table. You don't really expect to sit directly next to the likes of President Obama or Queen Elizabeth, although you wish you could, so you motion toward a seat farther down the table. As you pull out your chair to be seated, someone taps you on the shoulders and whispers in your ear, "The help and waitstaff are to report over there," and they point you to another room. The moment of a lifetime was just snatched from you in a flash. For a brief second, you were feeling on top of the world to be included with such an esteemed roster of people. Surely, there must have been a mistake. How could life be so unfair? Imagine the questions you could have asked President Obama had you only been sitting at the table. If only they had let you have your seat at least for hors d'oeuvres, then you would have humbly dismissed yourself and maintained some level of dignity and saved face. You could have gained so much insight from some of the top minds of this world, but now, completely deflated and exasperated, you are reduced to being just a servant—a nobody, it would seem. Or is it?

You'd think those who are great would be the ones sitting at that prestigious dinner table, waiting to be served by the likes of you and the rest of the help. However, Jesus turns His attention from the distinguished guests directly to you and the other servants and says, "The great ones are actually you all. Look at me. I'm here as one of the help too. I'm here to serve." The Galilean guru defines greatness by service. Those who serve others are the greatest. As you tie the apron around your waist and pick up a service tray, you ask yourself, "How is this greatness?" You've been reduced to a seemingly faceless, meaningless, and unimportant servant, working only for the pleasure of the guests and never to be seen or heard. I have asked myself, as well, one who is dedicated to ministry (which is service), how is this greatness? I realized that if I serve the table I am, therefore, responsible for bringing out utensils, food, and drink for those at the table. The truth of the matter is that I am directly responsible for what those guests will soon consume. Whatever I bring them is precisely what they'll have to eat. I'm in charge of their plates. They may not consider this during their dining experience, but those guests are forced to trust me, the lowly servant. They have no idea what I could have done to the food from the time it left the stovetop until it arrived at their sitting. I could have altered their food, added my own seasoning to it, and even, God forbid, spit in the food, and contaminated it. They do not know about any of this, but they do trust that I'll bring them their portions as ordered, prepared to their expectations. It is a great responsibility for the one who serves. If I bring out poison, then the guests will feast to their collective demises. If I bring out an outstanding entrée, then they will surely be delighted. The point of all this is not to get caught up in the power I have and can exert over the guests. Rather, I'm completely blown away at the great responsibility I have as a servant, and even more so, the level of trust. Not the level of trust the guests must have in me as I serve them, but the level of trust that the master of this banquet has in me. He trusts me with the responsibility to bring out precisely what He has prepared without adding to it or taking away. In full confidence, He loads my tray and sends me out to distribute the guests' plates. He puts the power of life and death in my hands and makes the conscious decision to trust that I won't hurt, harm, or kill any guest, but only serve each one with the best care. I think to myself, "Who am I that He would trust me so much, for I'm just a mere servant?" Yes, you're serving but you're more than a servant. You're a co-laborer with the head of this party. Ask yourself this question: Would I rather be honored and sit at the table, or would I rather be in honor and serve the table? What an honor to accept the responsibility and the trust of the Master. This is less concerned with my juxtaposition to the people, but my juxtaposition to the Master, the Creator. There is no need to even compare myself to anyone here, for I have the confidence, the trust, and the love of God. This is greatness, my friends.

6.2 You Are Much

"You shall love the Lord your God with all your heart and with all your soul and with all your might" Deuteronomy 6:5, (NASB). Is God really commanding His people to love Him? Shouldn't love be an organic decision made of one's free will? Let's save this question for another book and another day! There is plenty to unpack in this simple phrase, but let's focus on the last word concerning how we should love God—with all our might. The word strength could be used as well. Love the Lord your God with all of your strength. This is a common word transliterated from ancient Hebrew as *meod*, and it means much, muchness, force, abundance, and exceedingly. It can be used in simple everyday expressions, "Thank you very much/*tov meod*!" Let's reinsert the meanings of this elementary word back into the passage. In a literal translation, this verse can say, "Love the Lord your God with all your much." Love Him with all your muchness, your force, your abundance, and whatever you exceed in. The fulfillment of this verse is now contingent upon the reader because now you must recognize what are you much in. In which areas of your life are you exceedingly abundant and forceful? What about you is impactful? That is precisely what you use to express your love to God and ultimately to serve mankind. What are you passionate about? The great author, educator, preacher, and theologian Howard Thurman said, "Don't ask what the world needs. Ask what makes you come alive, and go do it. Because what the world needs is people who have come alive."[26] I am much in the area of music, empathy, and communicating the Word of God. Those are the areas of my life where I'm most forceful. It's what I'm good at.

This is extremely devotional at first glance, but Jesus challenged us to fulfill our devotion and love of God by extending that same love, treatment, and passion to each other. Love God and love your neighbor as yourself. Accordingly, it's critical that we are aware of what our much is and use it not just to align ourselves with the Almighty, but to mightily love His people as well. The uniqueness that is you—your gifts, your talents, and your abilities—is needed in this world to improve the lot of mankind and to better your community. What are you great at? To my college students, note the classes you most enjoy and feel most vivified when preparing for them. That's a good indication that subject is your field of passion as well.

I want to shout you out and encourage you. I dare you to offer no apology for being good at whatever you're good at. Sometimes people are mired in the mud of social comparison and can look at you with jealous eyes. It's so unfortunate that this happens. God is not Robin Hood. He does not steal from the rich to give to the poor. He doesn't have to take a single thing from your hand to bless mine. God is bigger than that. He's more blessed than that! He operates out of the bank of heaven with unlimited resources. Governments may shut down, but heaven is always open! No, you don't have to be ashamed of your talent or apologize for being gifted in a certain area. Do what you do and be amazing at it. Head up. Shoulders back. Chest out. Come alive and be great! Walk in whatever you're abundant in, and turn this world out for the better because of it. I'm speaking to your confidence and your self-esteem now. You are somebody, and the world needs you. You can't be much like anyone else, only your own much. Trust me, there is something you are much in. Take time to look into your heart and pray to discover what it is if you haven't yet.

Do you remember when the iPhone began to gain more popularity? This reminds me of an old iPhone 3 commercial from 2009 where the person holding the phone had random questions ranging from calories in food to the weather of the day, etc. The lone response to each inquiry was, "There's an app for that."

"Where did I park my car?" The response again, "There's an app for that!"

Apple was introducing the world to the millions of applications for all sorts of purposes, available at your fingertips to download at any time. In similar fashion, this world has millions of specific needs and inquiries, and I'm here to let you know that whatever they are, there's a MUCH for that! Whatever problems this world has, don't worry, there's a MUCH for that. The world needs you, and the world is waiting. You are great, and you are much! I give you permission to go ahead and tell everybody. Yes, you can tell everybody that you're the woman; you're the man!

6.3 Transformational Thinking about Greatness

As we continue to explore your muchness and greatness, I want to lift an example of what your greatness could be and challenge you to transform the way you think about it. I'm pushing you to go deeper into how you approach the way you view your life. I remember talking to a good friend about this subject, and I was urging him to look within to discover what he's good at and to consider his strengths. "What are you good at, man? What's your much?" He sat for a moment and searched the recesses of his heart for an answer. After an exasperated pause, he sheepishly said, "Well, I'm good at cleaning." His head hung low, and he barely made eye contact while answering. What I heard instead sounded more like, "What I'm good at is not good enough or significant. It's just cleaning." Perhaps he expected me to respond negatively to his seemingly humble suggestion: "Cleaning? That's all you can muster? You have a degree in communications and a ton of work experience, yet all you can do is clean?" I'm sure many of us have been here before; something you were good at or had a passion for wasn't valued in the eyes of someone else you cared about. I wanted him to be sure of his answer because I had a funny feeling my next words would surprise and empower him at the same time. "Cleaning? Final answer?" He hardly looked up and quietly said, "Yes." His body language was screaming defeat and disappointment. It was at this point the transformational moment set it.

Cleaning. When we hear cleaning, we may first associate it with cleaning a bathroom, scrubbing dirty toilets, sweeping floors, or vacuuming carpets. Through this lens, cleaning does seem pretty lowly. Let's zoom out from that perspective and view a broader picture. Let's think deeper. The bigger picture is that the person who cleans does more than just sanitize a toilet or scrub a floor, but such a person is an agent of restoration. To clean is to be an agent of restoration, rehabilitation, and organization. Your gift is not just to deodorize and make bathrooms look presentable. No. Your gift is to bring order and structure where there is chaos and clutter. Your ability to make things look new, to make them shine, to restore value, and to organize and give things their proper place for storage and display is simply yet, immensely put, godly! Godly? Yes, godly.

In the book of Genesis, the world that God created began as disordered chaos. It was dark, formless, without order or direction. God speaks to this raging tumult and says, "Let there be light," thus establishing order in the world. This tradition of establishing order from watery chaos is not exclusive to Judeo-Christianity, although that has its own unique nuances. Many creation narratives from the ancient Middle East all bear common elements of a watery chaos, and the god of the particular region or religion establishes order out of that chaos. You can find these prevalent themes in the Enûma Eliš of Ancient Babylon, the creation myths of various cities in ancient Egypt (Memphis, Thebes, Hermopolis, Heliopolis), and the Eridu Genesis of ancient Sumer. Many creation narratives also include stories of great floods and celestial battles between the gods—all to establish order in the world and bring an end to confusion and chaos. All of this demonstrates the impact of being a cleaner! It's deeper than what we may initially imagine, and now we can see through ancient history that its impact is substantial. Organization and order matters. Who would have ever thought that organizing would bear similarities to ancient creation stories that have been around for thousands of years? That is how important the cleaner's role is. Challenge yourself to think deeper and more critically of your much. Look at the root of what it is and not just the function. When you do this, I promise you'll see the need and the importance of your much and will be that much more endeared to deliver your worthy quantity of much to the world.

6.4 Insured Greatness

Just in case your confidence is still waning and you're not sure if you really are great, allow me to further prove you wrong. Let's say you have yet to discover what your much is and develop a plan to use it to benefit the world. That's okay. Self-discovery is a process and a state of mind–having the confidence in knowing you are significant. Perhaps you see others around you moving in their purpose and positively contributing to society, but you haven't quite found your own stride yet. Do not worry because the Great One set up an insurance policy for greatness. ". . . [G]reater is He who is in you than he who is in the world," 1 John 4b, (NASB). You have no choice but to be great, to be much, because God put a portion of Himself in you by way of His Holy Spirit. God is inexhaustible, and His attributes would take millennia to list. Yet He ensures we will be creative, influential, impactful, and exceedingly abundant in greatness because that is a measure of who He is. God can do anything but fail, and there's nothing too hard for Him. Therefore, regardless of how you feel about yourself and what you may or may not see right now, your only recourse is to be great. It's in you! Anything short of that is to deny who you really are and reject the greatness insurance policy already active in your life. You are great. You must be great. You are much, for He is much.

I speak to your confidence now. This is not arrogance or cockiness but merely a revelation of truth. For far too long, you've gotten away with self-deprecating comments. You've focused on your weaknesses and the areas of your life that are the least desirable. You're extremely familiar with your shortcomings and imperfections. Let's give that a rest and try something new: focus on where you are much.

I think back to the first NBA Finals matchup between the Cleveland Cavaliers and the Golden State Warriors in the summer of 2015. After a game five loss, LeBron James was asked about how much pressure he felt to carry his team because key players on his team were injured and unable to play. His response was one for the ages, "I feel confident because I'm the best player in the world. It's simple."[27] He was confident that his team could win the finals, even while undermanned, because they had the best player in the world: himself. Everyone is confident in their ability to win because of who they have on their team. "We got LeBron!" "We got Curry!" This chapter is called, "God's Got Me!" remember? When I say, "God's got me," I don't mean it in the sense of He has my back, and He'll be with me. No. I mean it in the literal sense. I am dedicated to the responsibility and honor of being in the service of the Master and serving His people, and I have identified the areas where I'm exceedingly abundant—much. I may even lack all the confidence necessary to impact the world in the manner I'm created to, but I still have a promise of greatness and much in me simply because God lives within me. I am confident that God's kingdom advances and that my community is positively impacted and blessed because God's got me. I'm on His team, and He has given me the game ball.

The same is true for you. You may not be a Hall of Fame basketball player or a Grammy award-winning musician, but you are the greatest YOU of all time. There will never be another you! You cannot be replicated, duplicated, or reproduced.

We all have an area of expertise and talent in our lives where we can say, "Nobody can compete with me in this arena. I own it!" We all have that special skill and/or specific niche in life where we can be as confident as LeBron was and take on the issues of wherever we live and work and resoundingly boom, "I feel confident because I am the best ________ in the world. It's simple." Your city, your school, your workplace: wherever you are, all will experience victory simply because you are there. God's got me! God's got you!

Chapter 7

The 50/50 Rule

Fifty percent of the time, mind your own business. The other fifty percent of the time, stay out of other people's business—*Jay T. Hairston, Sr.*

This is the 50/50 Rule created by my father, which was ingrained in us while growing up. When followed, it saved me from a lot of unnecessary trouble. When neglected, I immediately regretted my decision to not follow this wise rule. I now present you the secret of my childhood, adulthood, and even *now-hood* (yes, I made that up), the 50/50 Rule. Now, go obey it completely, and enjoy a healthy and productive life! Hush and do!

If only it were that simple, right?

7.1 There Is No Denying Our Interdependence

"No man is an island, entire of itself; every man is a piece of the continent, a part of the main" (John Donne).[28]

In highlighting the need for one another, the ancient Greek philosopher Plato concluded that cities and civilizations are formed because man is not self-sufficient alone.

> I think a city comes to be because none of us is self-sufficient, but we all need many things. Do you think that a city is founded on any other principle?
>
> No.
>
> And because people need many things, and because one person calls on a second out of one need and on a third out of a different need, many people gather in a single place to live together as partners and helpers. And such a settlement is called a city. Isn't that so?
>
> It is.

And if they share things with one another, giving and taking, they do so because each believes that this is better for himself? That's right.[29]

The apogee of our connectedness and interdependence as human beings is found in the sub-Saharan African philosophy of Ubuntu. It is a linguistic expression that denotes the philosophical/idealistic character of this region.[30] Ubuntu speaks to interdependence and prioritizes the well-being of the community over everything. This is not to have a communal well-being at the expense of an individual, but it is realizing that an individual's well-being is accomplished by pursuing the well-being of the community. David Lutz notes that the ethics of true community does not ask people to sacrifice their own good to promote the good of others but, instead, invites them to recognize that they can attain their own true good only by promoting the good of others.[31] The Kenyan-born Christian philosopher and writer, John Mbiti, in his seminal work, *African Religions and Philosophy*, expressed Ubuntu in his classic statement, "I am because we are; since we are, therefore I am."[32] In Ubuntu, we are successful only if we are successful. I am successful only if you are successful as well. We legitimize and authenticate our humanity within the context of community and not solely the individual. This is different from the Western culture value orientation of individualism. Why would I endorse such a foreign philosophy while I myself, and most of you, are likely Westerners?

This chapter is called "The 50/50 Rule," and you're anticipating reading about the necessity of minding your own business. Yes, that is a necessity, which I'll soon develop. Without a doubt, I will focus on the importance of staying in your lane, minding your own business, and focusing on what's ahead of you. Many can remember the 2016 Rio Olympics where Michael Phelps defeated his longtime rival Chad le Clos in the 200m butterfly final. Photographers caught a stunning photo where you actually can see South Africa's Chad le Clos looking over at Michael Phelps (USA) while finishing the race. It has served as a stunning reminder of the importance of focusing on the race ahead of you. However, I don't want to stress individual focus and lane-staying to the point where it completely excludes one of the most elemental parts of our humanity—our interdependence. I want to provide a reasonable balance of self-focus versus external focus.

The philosophy of Ubuntu is critical to *HushAndDo* because part of the reason you must get it done is that people are waiting for you and your gift. They are waiting for your answer and your skills. Again, I believe there is a you-sized void waiting to help improve mankind. Now let's explore our invaluable guideline for life, The 50/50 Rule and its application.

7.2 Minding Your Own Business and Social Comparison

There are many reasons why people mind other people's business. I'm sure you can think of plenty even as you've caught yourself at some point being mindful of someone else's business. Reasons for being nosey can include thinking you know better than someone else, rigid expectations, and an amplified sense of responsibility.[33] We feel we are qualified to intervene and give advice because we know better or have more experience than the other person. Therefore, we see the need to put in our valuable two cents. With rigid expectations, we have views of how things should be, and we expect everyone to conform to those norms. Lastly, an amplified sense of responsibility hints at the introduction to this chapter, our interdependence. We feel the social responsibility to interject and intercede where we see someone struggling or needing help. We simply can't ignore the child screaming for his or her mother lost in the grocery store. We pause and cringe as we witness an argument between a man and a woman escalate and get physical, rehearsing in our minds over and over whether or not we should intervene. We are concerned for their safety. It's a responsibility we feel. I accept all of these as reasons, but one, in particular, has captured my attention. It engages self-worth and identity. It can produce positive traits if not overdone. Unfortunately, I believe that, for many people, when this is used excessively, negative emotions are produced that are ultimately self-defeating and self-sabotaging. The "this" to which I refer is Social Comparison Theory.

Individuals compare themselves to others when they need an external standard against which to judge their abilities or opinions.[34] This is Social Comparison Theory in short. There are two types of this comparison: a downward and an upward comparison. The former is when we compare ourselves to someone we consider worse off than we are. For example, think of someone you graduated from high school with and how they seemingly haven't progressed in life. You are working full time, have started a family, and you're advancing in your career and constantly maturing. Your classmate, on the other hand, hasn't quite found his or her stride yet and is cycling through jobs and unstable income and doesn't appear to have a real plan for the future and hasn't quite secured his or her footing in life yet. The other is upward comparison, where we juxtapose ourselves to someone we think is doing considerably better than we are. Take the same high-school classmate scenario, but consider the classmate who went on to start a business, is doing very well, and lives in a house four times the size of yours. You get the picture. In a study on the dark side of frequent social comparisons, researchers posed the following: "People make social comparisons when they need to both reduce uncertainty about their abilities, performance, and other socially defined attributes, and when they need to rely on an external standard against which to judge themselves. The implication is that people uncertain of their self-worth who do not have clear, internal standards, will engage in frequent social comparisons."[35] Perhaps those same people are also battling false beliefs to which they subscribe as a result of deep wounding (Chapter 2). Can you see how this plays out in so many areas of our lives?

Let's be honest with ourselves here. I certainly had to. How many times have you gotten lost on Facebook or Instagram, looking at picture after picture, status after status? Everyone on your timeline has loads of content to post with their opinions and their activities. You look at each profile and each picture, and it appears everybody is doing so much and doing so well. I scroll and see that this musician has just finished a soon-to-be-released EP. A singer just finished recording vocals for her forthcoming album, and you see the studio pictures and hear audio snippets of her sessions. You read the status of the author who just found a publisher and is letting the entire Internet know his book will be printed soon. Your entrepreneur friend just shared a picture of him opening a new restaurant in your city, and you watch the video of him cutting the ribbon to launch his business. You glance with adoration at the pictures of the married couples on their dates and building their home together. You then scroll through the hundreds of announcements of what's to come, whether it's owning a business, earning a degree, or starting a new job. Suddenly you stop and ask yourself, "Well what in the world am I doing with *my* life?" All these people are doing wonderful things. Marriages are *perfect.* They're starting new careers, accomplishing their goals and dreams, making it happen, and living the American dream, while you struggle just to drag yourself to work that day. You ask yourself, "Am I the only one not doing anything productive with my life?" The feelings of insignificance arise as you continue to question yourself even more. You may not have realized it, but you have just done a series of upward social comparisons. Now, how will many of us respond to these timelines? What do we do? We go back through the timelines again, and we rethink everything we first saw. "It's about time he got that EP done. He'd been talking about it for several years now." We scroll to the next one. "Yeah, they're smiling in this picture, but they're just showing off. They aren't that happy!" Keep scrolling. "How's he going to open a restaurant, and all he's done is sell to-go dinners for years?" Can you see where I'm going? We aren't malicious, and we certainly wish nothing negative toward the people in our timelines pursuing their various endeavors, but for a second time, we have socially compared ourselves to them, only this time, it's downward. We want to feel better about ourselves and what we're doing, so we compare. There's a pitfall and danger to that.

I'm a big basketball fan, and I follow the NBA closely. On TNT's "Inside the NBA," you will often find recaps of the games from the previous day. What I've noticed and see so incredibly relevant to our conversation is that they rarely show the missed shots. Hardly ever will you find a network airing the lowlights unless you're watching "Shaqtin' a Fool." It's precisely the opposite! If they do show a jump shooter missing threes, it's only to highlight how he or she turned his or her night around and improved toward the end of the game. Social media is no different. Most of what we see, the pictures, the posts, the announcements, and the declarations, are all part of everybody else's highlight reel. Don't forget the pitfalls of declaring one's intentions publicly (Chapter 2)! We compare the NORMAL of our everyday life to the absolute BEST displays of everyone else! Do you see why there's such a disconnect and danger? We're not comparing normal and unfiltered with normal and unfiltered—but we're comparing normal and unfiltered with the best and highly filtered.

What are we threatened by in life? How does this keep us from moving forward? Where do you locate your identity? I've always argued that to anchor your identity in anything finite guarantees an eventual loss of identity one day. If your identity is rooted in your career and salary, then what happens if a life storm blows through, and you are no longer making the same amount of money you once were? This is especially critical for those in the business of people, whether social work, ministry, education, and counseling. If your identity is grounded in being there for people who rely on you, what happens when students graduate, and you're no longer needed at the rate you once were? There goes your identity as well. Our identity must be rooted in something deeper, greater, and stronger. I argue the best place to be informed of identity is by Christ and Christ alone. Until we locate our identity there, we will certainly continue to need external standards to judge and perceive ourselves. Social comparison is one of the many strategies used in the process of coping with threats, building resilience, and establishing our identity.[36]

This strategy of negative social comparison to make us feel better about ourselves only provides momentary comfort and relief for feeling unproductive, inadequate, and like everyone else is doing better than you are. It's not a long-term solution. It's fool's gold—just like the quick, short-term benefits we reap from anxiously announcing our moves to the world, especially in the absence of a concrete plan and the will to execute said plans. Downward social comparison can turn into a vicious cycle that will spiral deeper and deeper into negative emotions and thoughts. A study by Lyubomirsky and Ross in 1997 showed that happy and unhappy people are affected differently by social comparison.[37] When paired with a "better" peer, the sad people were more adversely affected by the comparison. Simply put, the happy people didn't pay much attention to how others were doing. However, the unhappy people quickly turned to more social comparisons to rescue themselves from their intense feelings due to being paired with a "better" peer.[38] More study needs to be conducted to explore the range of these negative emotions, but its conclusion remains clear. To be focused on what someone else is doing, in the long run, it's only to our own demise. This is why it is to your advantage to mind your own business 50 percent of the time and to stay out of others' business the other 50 percent of the time.

7.3 The Bright Side of Social Comparison

We have focused plenty on the negative aspects of frequent social comparisons, but not to the point where I will damn social comparisons as a whole. It's the frequent social comparisons that are destructive and overall negative. Such comparisons are the reasons that the message of this chapter is echoed repeatedly—obey the timeless 50/50 rule. You may now see that this is actually for your own benefit. Nevertheless, this remains a way to extract positive results from social comparison, which is inherently inescapable due to our worldwide interconnectedness. It all has to do with the approach. Social comparison has a bright side, which is integral to *HushAndDo*.

Curwen reports that in downward social comparison, there are two main reactions: contrast and assimilation.[39] If you contrast yourself with someone else who is doing worse than you are, this means you highlight the differences between you and that person. The result is a heightened self-esteem, which can lead to distancing yourself from that person and/or perceiving them condescendingly. The other reaction is assimilation. We move away from self-preoccupation, as assimilation focuses on the similarities between you and the other person. This births compassion, empathy, a willingness to help, and vulnerability. In 2014, I was privileged to plan an American tour here in Cleveland, Ohio, for friends in a gospel choir from Örnsköldsvik, Sweden (northern Sweden). One engagement on their itinerary was to sing at the Northeast Reintegration Center just outside downtown Cleveland. This government center aids in reintegrating women into society who have been locked up. Upon entering the facility and meeting the women, I couldn't help but realize just how familiar they all looked. They all appeared to be normal, everyday people. I believe we all have a certain perception and stereotype of what someone who's been incarcerated looks like. The people we met that day were so kind and loving. Some were older, and some were young. I saw people with warm hearts and hospitable spirits who could have easily been my grandmother, sister, teacher, college professor, pastor, etc. They looked no different than what we did. I remember asking myself silently, "What in the world happened that so many of these women ended up here? What could they have possibly done to merit a prison sentence and years later, end up here?" I remember a voice suddenly spoke to me saying, ***"The only difference between you and them is that you did not get caught!"*** You see, I didn't realize at the time that instead of looking down on them, I focused on our similarities. As a result, it engendered compassion for them. At that point, I couldn't judge their character or the costly decisions that had landed them in prison. All I had were feelings of empathy for them. I had a heart to help other women faced with arduous life circumstances that could cause them to do things that might get them in trouble. At the time, I was in my late twenties. I had graduated from high school in 2003, graduated from college in 2007, and earned a master's degree in 2013 and was recently married. Just like me, some of the women I met were in their late twenties, graduated the same year I did, and had families of their own beyond those four walls. In this context, assimilation produced softheartedness and empathy, which I believe are two core pieces that serve for the betterment of humanity.

There's still the matter of upward social comparison, with which we have yet to treat in detail. When we compare ourselves to someone we perceive is doing better than we are, it fosters feelings of helplessness, jealousy, and inferiority, which can jeopardize our identity.[40] Curwen goes on to highlight that persistence in this form of comparison has been found to lead to higher levels of burnout and defeat. There's no apparent benefit when comparing in this manner. There is a misconception that others enjoy a more emotionally fulfilling and enjoyable life than themselves, with plenty of research to support.[41] It's easy to assume that everyone else is doing better than you are, but this isn't necessarily true, even though that's how you may truly feel. This returns us to an aforementioned point: we watch everyone else's highlight reel and juxtapose that to our normal everyday-life reel. It's inconsistent, unfair, and, ultimately, we have no real way to measure the level of happiness and satisfaction in someone else's life. The solution, just like for downward social comparison, is upward assimilation. Find the similarities between you and the person to whom you're comparing that is doing better. Curwen, quoting Carmona et al., said, "Identifying common elements between the self and the 'better-offs' enables individuals to view their situations differently as they come to the conclusion that they are capable of mastering their difficult situations by building upon the common strengths they have and construct positive change."[42]

Instead of focusing on the differences between you and that person on your timeline who is "better-off," concentrate on what you have in common. I can choose to be depressed about the 2003 high-school graduate making millions of dollars, whose success would seem to eclipse mine completely, *or* I can focus on the simple fact that if he/she graduated, is married with children just as I am, then surely, it's possible for me to achieve the same level of success if not more! I won't win multiple NBA championships and have the same illustrious athletic career of LeBron James, a Black male who graduated from high school the same year I did and grew up just a few miles down the road in Akron, Ohio, (northeast Ohio). Even our birthdays are just seven December days apart, and he is married with children. We have much in common! Therefore, I can use this specific upward comparison as a launching point that pushes me to strive for greatness and to achieve it in all my fields of endeavor. The French philosopher and mathematician René Descartes coined the Latin phrase popular in philosophy, *cogito ergo sum*, which translates, *I think, therefore I am.* In a similar fashion, I have coined a phrase that I believe wholeheartedly, which has proven to be axiomatic in my own life: *video ergo est.* This translates, *I see it, therefore it exists.* If I can see it, conceptualize it, fathom, and/or imagine it, even in the deepest recesses of my mind, then it exists. If I can think it, then it has the potential for real-life existence. Many times, during our weekly forty-plus-minute-commute home from church when we served in East Cleveland, Christine and I would drive through the village of Bratenahl just to view its residential properties. Bratenahl is known for its luxurious and spacious homes along the shoreline of Lake Erie, which boasts some of the most beautiful houses we've ever seen. I'd slowly crawl my car down the street, allowing other traffic heading in my direction to go around us, so we could take in the amazing views. We would often get lost in the fantasy and imagine how we would decorate our home if we had one of those

Bratenahl-sized properties. As the years passed, and we grew in our marriage and careers, we noticed that what began as fantasy and playful imagination now felt more tangible, accessible, and possible. Once it was a dream, but now it has become an expectation, and we believe that one day it will be a reality for us. The size of the homes and their location didn't intimidate us. We saw it. We saw ourselves in it; therefore, it exists. For this reason, I endorse this approach to upward social comparison. ***When you are exposed to more than what you're familiar with, it opens the capacity of our mind's eye to achieve, see, and receive more.***

Years ago, in a sermon, Cleveland's most notable and active religious leader and pastor, Dr. R.A. Vernon, prayed not that the people of his church would be blessed and that God would provide more, but rather that they would be exposed to greater than what they've seen. As a result, they would have something more concrete to bring before God in their prayer time and personal aspirations.

7.4 50/50 Balance

The importance of the 50/50 Rule cannot be emphasized enough. There are pitfalls to including too many people in your business too soon. Check your motives and be honest as you evaluate your motives for bringing others into your fold. Yes, we are all interconnected and will need help from one another, but if your reason for including others in your business isn't for wisdom, advice, or assistance, then you may want to reconsider. Don't forget that millions of others are trying their best to keep the 50/50 Rule as well. Do them a favor, and keep them out of your business so they can focus on their own. Plus, you have so much to accomplish yourself.

I believe social comparison is one of the main reasons we can get caught up in another person's business. Whether intentionally or unintentionally, we see what others are doing and are inclined to compare ourselves. It happens about as automatically as our schemas and stereotypes do: the assumptions we quickly form about others based on what we see. The initial reaction may seemingly be unavoidable, but we can choose how we manage those instant reactions. If we indeed compare ourselves to others, we can choose to compare in a positive assimilating way that gives us a compassionate heart, encouragement, and hope. The effect of that method is twofold, as it benefits both you and other people at the same time. It's natural to want to measure yourself, and we often need a standard against which we can measure accordingly to assess progress. However, when overdone, it produces a negative effect and isn't healthy in the long run. Finally, it's time for an injection of truth-serum. Brace yourself. The reason you cannot afford to mind others' business is because you have plenty of your own to attend to.

As Queen Aoleon of Zamunda stated while dismissing her son's servant in the movie *Coming to America*, "Semmi, do you not have somewhere you should go?" Don't you have somewhere to go as well? Don't you have something you need to be doing instead of keeping tabs on everybody else? You have a great work ahead of you, and it can't be completed if you are preoccupied with other people's paths. To persist in concerning yourself with others' business instead of your own is to ultimately give in to a struggle that we all have in varying degrees. Roughly, 20 percent of the world's population deals with this, regardless of age, class, race, gender, or nationality—procrastination.

You've put it off long enough and delayed as much as you could. No more! I'm coming over to perform the funeral and burial services for the procrastination in your life.

Chapter 8

Procrastination

Dirge (dûrj), n. a song or poem in commemoration of the dead.

This chapter will be the dirge for procrastination as well as several popular misbeliefs about it. We're delivering a swift deathblow to it all now.

◈◈◈

Tomorrow. I'll give my life tomorrow. I thought about today, but it's so much easier to say tomorrow. Who promised you tomorrow? Better choose The Lord today. For tomorrow very well might be today—The Winans.[43]

Hush and Do

How ironic to leave the chapter about procrastination until nearly the end of this book? It's time we talked about it and treated it. Many books have been written, researched, and published to cover the gamut of procrastination; therefore, this chapter is merely cursory, scratching the surface of the issue. Psychologists Joseph Ferrari, Tim Pychyl, Walter Mischel, and Roy Baumeister are the leading experts in this area, and I stand on the shoulders of their research to present some unique perspectives on procrastination. The Winans song above and the poem below are suitable to frame our discussion as we finally tackle the ardent adversary, vile villain, and nefarious nemesis of many—procrastination.

He Had a Year to Do It In *by John Lea*

He had a year to do it in

So brushed the thought away,

A chap with half his energy

Might do it in a day.

A year! 'Twas too ridiculous,

As everyone should find;

However, he would get it done

And have it off his mind.

But not today. A few months hence would suit him better still;

Meanwhile, a far less irksome job

Might occupy his skill.

He would not let the matter pass

Entirely from him, No;

And doubtless he might take it up

In, say a month or so.

He had six months to do it in!

For six long months had flown;

Well, why should that alarm a chap

With talents like his own?

The job, whence once embarked upon,

Would soon be rattled through;

However, he would think of it,

In, say, a week or two.

He had three months to do it in!

"Oh brother!" was his cry;

The thing hangs on me like a weight,

Each day that passes by.

Let's see: three months? Ah, that's enough,

But, just to clear the doubt,

Make arrangements for a start

Before the month is out.

He had a week to do it in!

And care was in his glance.

"It's hard," he cried, "that flight of time,

Won't give a chap a chance!"

He still delayed, the swift week passed,

As weeks will ever run,

And though a year was given him,

The task was still undone. [44]

To procrastinate is to defer or delay action. The etymology of the word *procrastination* literally means to *put off until tomorrow* or *belonging to tomorrow.* It is the gap that exists between intention and action. It becomes a more serious problem when the gap in time between hatching an intention and actually starting or finishing a certain behavior increases.[45] Hours become days. Days become weeks. Weeks become months. Months become years. And what you intended to do still has not been initiated or completed.

There's one glaring issue with procrastination, before we even go any deeper—tomorrow is not promised! Why would you put something off until tomorrow, or next week, or next month, or next year even that you could do or begin to do today? How are you so confident that you will be around tomorrow or next year? Certainly, at the time of writing this book, I believe that I have many more years ahead of me than I do behind me. In my brief stint on Earth, I have learned that the invincibility of youth is a fallacy. When I was younger, it was almost impossible to conceive of getting older and dealing with the issues that come with aging. I foolishly believed "it" would never happen to me. The "it" meaning the vicissitudes of life, such as tragedy, loss, hard times, setbacks, and the like. I see it now, like King Solomon when he said, "Again I saw that under the sun the race is not given to the swift, nor the battle to the strong, nor bread to the wise, nor riches to the intelligent, nor favor to the skillful; but time and chance happen to them all," Ecclesiastes 9:11 (New Revised Standard Version). As I amass more yearly revolutions around the sun,

I have observed life and this world, and I'm realizing with my own eyes that Father Time is truly undefeated. Getting older occurs automatically as long as breath remains in the body. Growth, maturation, and evolution are a choice I must make today. Time will do what it has always done since its inception: advance and wait for no one. This is the truth of time, and it won't change until the Creator of time appoints time to take its final breath. So many people associate procrastination with poor time management. "I wish there were more hours in a day!" "I need more time!" "I have to manage my time better!"

Don't focus on managing your time. Focus on managing yourself, and time will manage itself.

Let's be clear about a few things. Procrastination is not about having fun, as many would like to think it is. Whether you accept it or not, procrastination affects your future self as well as others (secondhand procrastination). Lastly, everything boils down to, as Dr. Pychyl describes, "the feel-good." Everything in procrastination points to finding ways to feel good.

8.1 The Fake: The Misconceptions about Procrastination

"Everyone procrastinates, but not everyone is a procrastinator."[46] Surely, at some point in all of our lives, we have procrastinated, but there is a difference between having procrastinated and being a chronic procrastinator—one who regularly self-sabotages by welcoming distractions and choosing to avoid and/or put off to that non-guaranteed tomorrow, today. I can already imagine many of your thoughts: "It's probably more prevalent with those millennials!"[j] "You already know it's nothing but indecisive women who are the main procrastinators!" I'm tempted to believe that myself, as I'm a witness to the difficulty that frequently arises when I ask the women in my life this simple question, "What would you like to eat?" And all the men reading this said, "Amen." I'm sure

---

[j] May we please, if just for one moment, stop putting down millennials, whom I happen to be one myself! An old one, but a millennial nonetheless. We have contributed many great things to society and to this planet. Thank you!

my international friends observing our American entertainment-driven society are thinking that procrastination is definitely an American thing. However, all of the above assumptions are false! Research has shown that roughly 20 percent of the world's population are chronic procrastinators. This percentage spans across all ages, all races, nationality, socioeconomic status, and all levels of education. It's not a young people's problem, or a gender-specific problem, or a rich-and-poor problem. It is a *worldwide human problem. But* there is hope and help. Again, procrastination is the gap that exists between intention and action. It's the space and time between something one sets out to do and the completion of that task. It becomes more problematic as the distance between starting and finishing increases.

8.2 Under Pressure Thrill Seekers

"I work better under pressure!" I'm sure many of you have either heard this statement before, have uttered it, or even worse, truly believed it! I will not deny that sometimes things can turn out well when working under pressure. I have submitted a few "under pressure" papers—seconds before a deadline and fortunately received a good grade. That is the exception and not the norm. Studies reveal that working under pressure, in fact, increases the likelihood for errors of omission and commission. It ultimately results in producing less and completing fewer tasks than those who don't work under pressure.[47] Let's apply these findings logically to a real-life situation: You have a report for work due by five o'clock before the office closes for the day. The work isn't challenging, and it bores you. You began writing it only thirty minutes ago, attached it to the email, and clicked send seconds before the clock changed to five. Congratulations! You technically got the report in on time, but did you have time to review your work? Did you check your work more than just relying on the discouraging red scraggly line underneath misspelled words in Microsoft Word? Undergrad and graduate students, this could easily be you too! The thrill you seek, thus, why you procrastinate until the last minute, is a product of your lack of interest and being easily distracted. You don't need the thrill to do good work. You welcome the thrill to stave off your boredom. Not only that, but is it really a thrill? I have to pause and ask myself that very question as I struggle with the false belief of thrill-seeking/working-best-under-pressure form of procrastination. I remember the first time I flew to Sweden to be the featured guest artist for a gospel music festival in the northern city of Örnsköldsvik. The gracious festival director and the church hosting the festival sent for my father and me, and they were bubbling with anticipation for my inaugural arrival. I always thought I enjoyed the thrill that came with cutting the time close until it nearly cost me the entire trip. Most international airports recommend that you arrive at least two hours before your flight's takeoff when traveling out of the country. Being my usual self, and not taking seriously the consequences of arriving late to the airport, I finally dragged myself in with roughly 45 minutes to spare. I already knew my father was seething with frustration as evidenced by how little he had to say when I arrived. If my father has little to say, then *you know* he's pretty vexed! His look said it all. I'm thinking to myself, "You really did it this time, Jay. You guys will miss your flight." The agents are giving us the "You probably won't make this flight" look of doubt as we approached to check our luggage. I believe they moved with deliberate sloth because they believed missing the flight was a foregone conclusion. We were flying out of

Cleveland to Chicago, where we would board the overseas flight to Stockholm, Sweden. We would then board a connecting flight to our final destination up North. My procrastination, which I classified as thrill-seeking, would have indeed cost us the entire trip had it not been for a small error in our boarding passes. My father and I have the same name. The only difference is that I am the second edition of Jay Timothy Hairston, better known as Jay Timothy Hairston II. The tiny omission of the suffix II in the end prevented us from ever boarding. Thankfully, the festival heard of our mishap and sent two more tickets for later that day. We eventually got to Chicago to board another overseas flight, but to Copenhagen, then to Stockholm, and then to Örnsköldsvik. Here is the cold truth that I now sadly realize: we were going to MISS that flight one way or another! It just happened to work out in my favor that there was an error with the boarding passes. I immediately threw United under the bus to save my own hide from the disappointment, wrath, and eventual lecture from my father. Once again, I was late and tempted fate. I could finally relax and let out the proverbial sigh of relief once we took off later that evening. "See! We're good, Good Brotha!" (one of my nicknames for my father is the Good Brotha). As I grinned, I realized being on that flight was the equivalent of hitting a full-court shot as the clock expired in overtime, and we were down three: luck! It felt good to be on that aircraft; although, I was squeezed between two husky men whose height and corpulent flesh both exceeded my own!

It was another successful close call in the books. I wrestled with fate and won again, and it felt good. I felt like I had won the championship, and I was crowned the most valuable player. I now realize it wasn't a thrill I was experiencing after all. The time from my arrival at the airport until we finally departed was filled not with feelings of excitement and joy, but rather with feelings of dread, uneasiness, and high stress! The success of boarding the airplane stopped my prodigious panicking. I had been incorrectly calling it a thrill this whole time, and perhaps you too have mislabeled the times you've elected to procrastinate. The "thrill" is not a thrill at all but only the relief from the anxiety, the distress, the worry, and foreboding of possibly missing the deadline, or, as in my case, my flight!

8.3 The Planning Fallacy

Planning fallacy is an occurrence where estimates about the time required to complete a future task demonstrate an optimism bias, thus underestimating the actual time needed to complete the task. In other words, one has an unrealistic assessment about how much time is necessary to get something done. For example, someone has a ten-page research paper due at midnight but thinks beginning the paper at 11 p.m. will be more than enough time to complete it. His or her optimism is clearly unrealistic and strained, and, in most cases, one hour will not be enough time to start and complete a research paper.

At times, we have all underestimated the amount of time needed to get something done. The assumption is that procrastinators do this to a much greater extent. To test this, researchers examined the study habits of university students.[48] It's commonly believed that procrastinators just have terrible time management. Hand them a planner, and they should be cured if they use it, right? This is incorrect. Giving a procrastinator a planner hoping they will abandon their delaying ways is about the same as telling someone who struggles with depression to "Cheer up!" It just doesn't work that way. Students were to submit estimates of their study plans for eight days prior to two midterm exams. Afterward, these estimations were compared to the time they logged in for actual studying. Students who were rated as high in procrastination did not demonstrate an optimism bias for study time. Granted, those procrastinating students did study at a later time and studied less than those low in procrastination. However, regardless of the level of procrastination, both groups of students accurately predicted how much time they would need for studying, and their study logs mirrored their predictions. The students knew what their study habits were, and the high procrastinators, when estimating how much time they would need for study, factored in their procrastination habits as well! The study also revealed a surprising result as students scoring high in procrastination were actually slightly better at meeting their study time predictions than those scoring low in procrastination. The students who were high procrastinators obviously studied less than students who were low procrastinators, but they also predicted that they would study less. Overall, this study displayed that procrastinators have no problem with telling time and estimating how much time is needed to accomplish a task. Their ability to manage time isn't inherently distorted because they procrastinate. Therefore, addressing time management itself may not be the direct answer to cure your procrastination because that, ultimately, isn't the root of your problem. Many will view procrastinators as people who waste time, but with them, it is not truly time wasted, but rather time valued in different ways. We choose to entertain the distractions, and we choose to delay. In my estimation, it boils down to two things: feeling good now and self-regulation.

8.4 The Feel Good

Here is where the work of ending procrastination becomes incredibly personal and demands your honesty. Part of procrastination is short-term mood repair. As earlier stated, it's all about giving in to the feel-good. The feel-good is whatever pleases us in the moment and keeps us in our seemingly happy place. It is a deceitful utopia where we keep ourselves shielded from being challenged, pushed, stretched, or drawn away from our comfort zones. The more we give in to it and procrastinate, the more time reveals that what felt like utopia was actually a miserable dystopia where we had completed nothing that we had intended and are, now, laden with unfinished work.

We have all faced having to do things we don't want to do, whether it's an earnings report we don't enjoy graphing, an imminent change in diet, beginning an exercise routine after you've been inactive for months, confronting a difficult situation, or a change in work hours. What happens when these examples and procrastination meet? We experience negative emotions when thinking about the undesired task. It's the anxiety, the release of adrenaline, norepinephrine, and cortisol you feel when you must have that difficult discussion with a co-worker to address something you don't like. It's the letdown you experience when you realize that overindulging in sweets is indeed not the path toward weight loss, and you have to give them up for a season. Therefore, to reduce the negative feelings, we avoid the task, thus feeling better. We procrastinate whatever we have to do to escape the discomfort of going through with it. Dr. Pychyl identified this behavior as "negative reinforcement." For example, it's cold outside, so I put on a coat. Putting the coat on removes the negative variable, me being cold.[49] When we do this, we are giving in to the now, to the moment; we are giving in to the feel-good. See how this works with things we've already addressed, namely fear. I repeat, the only way past is through.

Critical to the notion of the feel-good is delayed gratification. Delaying and waiting are not necessarily procrastination in and of themselves, but they usually accompany any journey toward achievement. "With procrastination, you are working hard not to have something happen. With waiting, you are preparing for the next step—you are working toward a goal, not avoiding one."[50] The feel-good always wants it now. It wants success now. It wants pleasure now. It wants everything *right now*, in this moment. But that's not realistic. Sometimes it's necessary to delay gratification for a greater good. The renowned social psychologist Walter Mischel conducted the Marshmallow Test in which he tested children's ability to delay gratification. He placed a marshmallow in front of each child and gave him or her the option to eat the marshmallow there in that moment or to wait awhile. If the child chose to wait, he or she was rewarded with more marshmallows in addition to the original one. Mischel took note of the children who gave in to the now versus the children who waited. He followed them into their adulthood, monitoring their progress in life. The children who resisted eating the lone marshmallow went on to achieve higher levels of education and earn higher salaries than their counterparts who immediately ate it.

Critical to overcoming procrastination is our ability to recognize our tendency for the feel-good and choosing to overcome it and to resist the temptation to give in to the now. No doubt, resisting temptation in many cases is an ongoing and unpleasant exercise. I'm not calling you to be robotic. I realize that, at times, the strength to resist will fluctuate as you battle the impulse to allow distractions and procrastinate. It seems that life waits for more opportune moments to present its distractions, as if it knows exactly the right time to show up. As soon as you begin working on your task, here comes the temptation to be distracted and lose focus. Remember this—it's not that the impulse to wander off is irresistible—it's the combination of that impulse showing up during a moment of weakened self-control and willpower, which psychologists refer to as self-regulation.

8.5 Self-Regulation Failure

A legend of the French Industrial Revolution purports that peasant workers wore wooden clogs for shoes. The French word for this shoe, associated with the lower class and poor people, is *sabot*. Frustrated workers purposefully jammed their wooden shoes, or their *sabots*, into the gears of the machinery to stop production and to ultimately destroy it. These and other rebels were known as *saboteurs*. Those who damaged property were labeled enemies of the state, and their acts were known as *sabotage*. Fast-forwarding to today, when someone intentionally destroys their path to success, regardless of the task at hand, psychologists refer to it as *self-sabotage*.

People who procrastinate, whether they realize it or not, intentionally place obstacles in their path to inhibit the completion of any work or activity. It sounds crazy to hear it this way, but it is the truth. If you procrastinate, then it is *you*—not time, not external forces, not deadlines, not assignments, not responsibility or expectation, and not anyone or anything else—you are the harbinger of your own demise. Consider the college student who sits down to write a paper that's due before midnight.

It's already 9 p.m., and she's only written a page and a half, yet the paper needs to be ten pages at least. As she prepares to write, her cell phone is sitting next to her laptop, and she's ready to respond to any phone call or text she may get. She placed it there herself, nobody else! As she begins to write, her phone chimes to let her know someone just shared her Facebook post. A few minutes later, her Instagram story from earlier in the day is beginning to rain with commentary. She then decides to update the world on her current plight and tweets, "Gotta get this paper done!" She sets her phone down to begin writing again, only to be interrupted by her phone again a few seconds later—Snapchat. Has anyone forced her to respond to the text messages? Is she being coerced into monitoring her Instagram and Facebook accounts? Of course not! The immediate distraction in that moment—that, ever available information-processing, global social-communication device, which is her cell phone—was placed by her side by choice.

Roy Baumeister's overview of self-regulation failure presents the core "ingredients" of self-regulation.[51] The first attribute deals with standards, which are ideals, goals, or other conceptions of possible states. Without clear and consistent standards, self-regulation will be hampered. You must have a destination before you take off, and you must know where you're going and what you want to do. Have clearly defined goals and aspirations, and then you may pursue. The second ingredient is monitoring. You must keep track of your activity between intention and action. You must monitor your states as well as your actions. The third set of "ingredients" are feedback and change. After you've monitored your state and your actions, if you have fallen short of your desired outcome, you must change the state. You have to do something different, or you can die slowly.

Does willpower exist in an inexhaustible amount or can it be depleted with frequent usage? These are questions that psychologists have argued for years. Willpower is the key component to overcoming procrastination and most of the obstacles in our lives as it relates to the movement of *HushAndDo*. It enables us to override habits and alter the way we typically respond. Baumeister compares self-regulation and the willpower to execute to the way athletes use their bodies to perform in their respective sports. Each person's capacity for self-regulation appears to be a limited resource, which is renewable over time and can be increased or decreased as a result of gradual developments or practice.[52] One person cannot regulate everything at the same time. I find this approach to understanding self-regulation and willpower to be the most practical. For months, I would stay out of the gym due to not prioritizing exercise. Suddenly, I would get the urge to return to my workout routine, which usually included much weightlifting sprinkled with a few dashes of cardio. Believe it or not, in my senior year of college, my max for bench press was 315 pounds. I thought that was impressive for a creative church boy and performing-arts fanatic who wasn't an athlete! Reminding myself of this and wearing it as a badge of honor and respect, I would return from my quarterly hiatus to resume lifting and conquering the gym. However, I quickly learned that if I'm not doing anything to maintain my muscle, eventually I'll lose it. In the same regard, if you are not exercising your muscles of self-control and discipline, then self-control and discipline will begin to deteriorate. The good news is that, just like the muscles in our bodies, we can build up and strengthen our capacity for self-regulation. There may be moments where stressors are pressing in on every side and temptation is quickly amassing around you. According to the information presented, you may conclude that once you've exhausted your reserves for self-control and willpower, you will be highly susceptible to giving in to the temptations/distractions. If you're a Los Angeles Lakers fan, you have seen plenty of games where Kobe Bryant has had to play excessive minutes and remain on the court even when he's clearly exhausted. For some reason, he, like many other champions, can will himself to find the energy and strength needed to finish a game and remain effective to lead his team to victory. He may hit a wall, but he finds a way to dig even deeper and deliver for his team. In the same manner, even when situations seem to have completely drained our self-control, we, like the champion athletes, can still summon willpower and will ourselves to victory over whatever temptations we may encounter. Yes, we can!

8.6 Physics and Self-Control. Yes, Physics!

Inertia—the property of matter by which it retains its state of rest or its velocity along a straight line so long as it is not acted upon by an external force.[k]

It's easier to maneuver inertia than it is to stop it. Simply stated, it's easier to change the direction of motion and momentum than it is to completely bring it to a halt. That is why many driving schools teach its students to be alert and lean more toward steering out of the way to avoid accidents than relying heavily on the brakes to achieve the same thing. Although inertia is a term from physics, there is a similarity between it and psychological processes. It's like a train with many cars. We encounter a certain stimulus, and it sets a series of thoughts in motion, and those thoughts lead to a response, and the response leads to a consequence. What can be done to alter the way these processes actuate in life? For example, let's go back to the

---

[k] "Inertia." *Random House Webster's Dictionary*. BallentineBooks, 2001.

student who begins to study for the exam with her phone sitting right in front of her. She begins studying. Her phone rings. She reads the text message. The text message makes her think of someone else she had to respond to. She responds to the person. Afterward, per her habit, she does her hourly cycle through all her social media outlets: Instagram, Snapchat, Facebook, and Twitter. After completing the cycle, she sets the phone down and resumes studying, only for the phone to ring again! That is just an example of how this train of psychological processes works. Identify your train! You know what triggers your distractions, and you also know what it takes to focus and lock in on a particular task. Wouldn't it be easier for her to just put the cell phone away rather than be forced to stop her social-media cycle? Eliminate the distraction at the root.

What does this have to do with inertia and self-control? It's easier to maneuver that train of thinking and response than it is to stop it. Allow me to use another example to tie it all together. If your self-regulation goal is to practice abstinence, one of the greatest ways to achieve that goal is to shut down any sexual advancement after the first kiss versus engaging in foreplay for an entire hour and then suddenly trying to stop. Good luck with that! If your goal is abstinence, then you increase your strength by changing direction earlier rather than later. Stop at first base. If first base puts you in the frame of mind to round all the bases and head home, then don't even go to first base. What sets this train in motion? It is the things to which we pay attention.

Research has found over and over that managing attention was the most common and often the most effective form of self-regulation. Conversely, attention is usually the precursor to self-regulation failure. Whatever triggers you to lose control and procrastinate can be averted early on by managing your attention. Perhaps you could fix your eyes on something greater.

"Therefore, since we are surrounded by so great a cloud of witnesses, let us also lay aside every weight and the sin that clings so closely, and let us run with perseverance the race that is set before us, looking to Jesus the pioneer and perfecter of our faith, who for the sake of the joy that was set before [H]im endured the cross, disregarding its shame, and has taken his seat at the right hand of the throne of God," Hebrews 12:1-2 (NRSV).

Jesus resolutely set out for Jerusalem, the place where His destiny would be fulfilled. Waiting ahead of Him were opportunities to teach and speak in parables, confronting the religious elite, challenging the status quo of His day, healing the sick, performing miracles. He also faced betrayal, abandonment, trial, flogging, and the eventual brutal execution by way of Roman crucifixion. There is no doubt that this would have His attention and keep Him in perpetual agony for the days to come. This was the reality of His path, yet despite the enormity of His suffering, He endured it all, disregarding the shame of being put to death naked for all to see.

How so? For the joy that was set before Him. I believe, that joy was in realizing that His sacrifice meant salvation, redemption, and restoration for the entire world. He focused on something beyond His immediate state. He saw something bigger, locked eyes on it, and used that image to get through everything else He had to endure to accomplish his mission. He controlled what He paid attention to. Using that focus, He was also able to disregard giving in to the feel-good for the sake of accomplishing His mission. Psychologists refer to this form of self-regulation and attention control as transcendence. Likewise, it is possible for you to press beyond the boundaries of ordinary limits. What do you want more than anything, and how does that prioritize compared to the rest of your wants? Lock in on the big picture, and if that consumes your attention, the rest can more easily fall in place. You can transcend too. You have to for the sake of your work, your goals, and your responsibility to mankind. The brothers of Alpha Phi Alpha Fraternity Inc.® said it best, "First of all, servants of all, we shall transcend all."

8.7 The Real: The Truth about You and Procrastination

Procrastination is not beyond your control. You have the power to determine your course of action each day. Yes, temptations and distractions will arise and attempt to unhinge your focus and redirect your attention, but you do not have to be a slave to these temptations. Reclaim your power, and take control of how you use your time.

Some reasons for procrastination are deeper issues of the heart. I invite you to continue on the inward journey with me, and take an honest look at yourself. This won't be comfortable, but it will be healthy and beneficial. I cannot dictate how real you will be with yourself, but I can guarantee no power or entity can keep you from taking this critical self-assessment. What are you afraid of? Fear and procrastination go hand in hand. Consider me as an example. I was a Spanish major at Baldwin-Wallace College (now Baldwin Wallace University). In my freshmen year, I was privileged to become good friends with a fellow freshman from Ponce, Puerto Rico, named Edgar. I had been studying Spanish for five years by this point, but all the rules of grammar and verb conjugation, which I religiously maintained, did not translate well to having an everyday conversation and understanding spoken-Spanish from native speakers. He mostly only spoke to me in Spanish, and often I interpreted for him when we went out. I have this fear of failure that can certainly get the best of me at times. For me, being a successful Spanish-speaker meant I could speak to a native Spanish speaker without speaking a word of English. Not only that, the most rewarding benchmark of success was when I was asked the golden question at the end of the conversation, *"¿Dónde naciste y de donde viene tu familia?*

(Where were you born and where does your family come from?) *¿Eres Dominicano, no?"* (You're Dominican, right?). The feeling of speaking well in a foreign language was so satisfying, but my fear of mispronouncing a word or having a weak accent that exposed my Americanness often overwhelmed me. I was afraid to get laughed at—that native speakers would think I couldn't carry a conversation in their language, and that they would resort to speaking to me in English. Such was the hallmark of failure. Allowing that fear to dictate my actions, I found ways to avoid Spanish speakers I knew. I had so many successful conversations in the past, but what if the next one didn't go as well? What if the next person used words with which I wasn't familiar? What if we got into a topic of discussion where I was deficient in its vocabulary? To cope with this, I would pretend to be sick during those moments. My advisor, the late Dr. Maria Marín, to whom I was close, was from San Juan, Puerto Rico, and the thought of disappointing her by saying a single word incorrectly haunted me. I wanted to impress her and make her proud. This was self-induced pressure. She was the kindest woman and understood that I was in the throes of learning the language. I was intentionally delaying and putting obstacles in front of the very thing I needed to achieve the very thing I desired—to earn a degree in Spanish and to be fluent in it!

How has fear produced procrastination in your life? Do you witness familiarities in your own life from reading about mine? I needed hours and hours of dialogue and discussion in Spanish, yet I deliberately put it off because of my fear. Not just my fear of erring, but fear of compromising my social reality—to risk altering people's perception of who I was and my capabilities. This is also known as social esteem. I absolutely love it when people think I am Colombian, Puerto Rican, or Dominican. This isn't because of a lack of pride to be an African-American male, but it's the stamp of approval that tells me I'm speaking Spanish well. It made me feel good to be celebrated as the resident linguist and language expert among my peers and family. Being seen as smart and multitalented became a part of my identity, and I longed for the attention of that perception as I silently struggled with doubt. Am I as smart as they think I am? Am I really multitalented, or do I just have a few decent tricks up my sleeves to make people think I am truly talented? Do these sound like questions you've asked yourself as well?

8.8 The Perfectionist Procrastinator

This point leads me to another area of procrastination that I must expose so you can get free—perfectionism. Pychyl gives two flavors of perfectionism. The first is the self-oriented perfectionist. This is the person who simply loves to do things well and perfectly, nice and neatly, with no mistakes. The second flavor is the socially prescribed perfectionist—who most of us are like regarding the battle with procrastination—who is concerned with living up to other people's standards. The socially prescribed perfectionist usually has a lot of negative internal talk and procrastinates more often than the former. Your motivation is external: the perceptions and opinions of others. It is difficult to accept this truth, but you must overcome it and get better. Being a perfectionist keeps us safe from criticism and failure to meet up to other's standards for us. "The perfectionism of procrastinators is motivated by a desire to belong and be liked by others; they justify their procrastination by saying that delays will result in a better outcome."[53] On the other hand, the self-oriented perfectionist delays to produce the best product possible regardless of what others think. I cannot answer this question for you. You must be honest with yourself. What is your motivation? You don't need to use a cloak of perfectionism to disguise that you're a procrastinator. Let's come out of hiding and confront ourselves and the truth. For example, the socially prescribed perfectionist has a due date pending for a report at work. He usually produces great work and wonderful presentations, and the entire office knows he's one of the best, but he's nervous about this particular report. He desperately requests an extension to the deadline, claiming he needs more time to get it just right. He disguises his procrastination with being a perfectionist, but really, he's concerned that his work won't be the same quality as it's been before and that the rest of his co-workers will notice it too. Therefore, to protect himself and his social identity (his co-workers' belief that he's the best) he puts everything off and procrastinates. Does that sound like anybody you know? Like you? Ferrari directly asserts that when you claim you can't finish a task because you are a perfectionist, you're really telling the world you want to protect your social esteem—you need to have others feel good about you.[54]

8.9 Let's Move Forward

How has remaining safe, staying in your comfort zone, and submitting to the feel-good, benefited you as you consider your goals and intentions? Yes, procrastinating is easy, and transforming into a new life of productivity will be difficult at first, but it's a muscle that can be worked out and strengthened. It's time to hit the mental gym! It's time to activate the champion inside of you to dig deep and strive for what is yours—your success! Locate your inner Michael Jordan, your inner Serena Williams, or your inner Muhammad Ali, and command yourself to come forth as a champion. You can overcome all odds and become what you're supposed to be. I understand the fear that accompanies success and failure. I accept your humanity and empathize with you in your journey. There are things of which I yet remain fearful, but I have to take the next step forward despite that fear. The fear cannot paralyze me, and it cannot paralyze you! Identify what is causing you to procrastinate. To find a solution, you need to know what is motivating your tendency to delay. Does fear of failure or success make you avoid beginning or finishing a task? Or are you hooked on the adrenaline rush of trying to beat a deadline because you are easily bored? Are you concerned with how others see you, so you front to be a perfectionist? Are your willpower and self-regulation muscles frail and debilitated? Transparency and self-assessment are highly critical to overcome procrastination. I want to encourage and empower you with a few things that help me overcome my tendency to procrastinate.

"God blessed them, and God said to them, 'Be fruitful and multiply, and fill the earth and subdue it; and have dominion over the fish of the sea and over the birds of the air and over *every living thing* that moves upon the earth" Genesis 1:28 (NRSV). In this verse, God is primarily referring to all the animals and their domains: land, sea, and water. In the context of self-regulation, I have decided to extend the meaning of this verse to cover myself as well. Biologists would classify human beings in the animal kingdom and in the class of mammals, as we are warm-blooded beings. By no means am I trying to refer to humankind or myself as an animal, but pertinent to the emphasis I added in Genesis 1.28, I would be classified as a living thing that moves upon the earth. We are to subdue the earth and have dominion, authority, and control over everything on this terrestrial ball, including ourselves! It amazes me how often we seek to dominate and control every facet of our lives yet seemingly exclude self-control and self-domination. I use this small verse to remind myself of who's in charge here. I am. The boss is not procrastination and the myriad distractions it seeks to find when I endeavor to complete tasks. The ruling authority is not external but rather internal. It's me. It's you. Take your authority and walk in it. You can overcome procrastination. You can overcome yourself.

In addition to reminding myself of my inherent authority, I also place values before me to refocus when tempted to be distracted and put off something I could do today. Everything has a value, whether objective or subjective. When confronted with the temptation to procrastinate, I place two values before me and choose. What do I value more: the success that will come with finishing this book and being able to help others or watching a YouTube video and having a quick laugh? Place the values in front of you when it comes to weight loss when confronted with the opportunity to enjoy a treat that's counterintuitive to your dieting goal. What's worth more right now: enjoying the sugary sweetness of this treat or my overarching goal of weight loss? When you place the values before you, it paints a clearer picture and the greater good. It allows you to transcend the immediate moment and delay instant gratification.

Perhaps your goals are too abstract. Dream immensely, set lofty goals, and think big and outside the box concerning the things you want in life. However, research has shown that where there is a lack of concrete definition for any task or assignment, procrastination can likely follow. Furthermore, distant events tend to be represented more abstractly while things closer to the present are represented more concretely. Early in the year, you plan to go on a family cruise for Christmas. In January and February, the cruise itself is abstract. It's a cruise, and you'll board the boat and have an amazing time. However, come early December, you're thinking about that cruise in more concrete terms: what to pack, where to park the car while you're gone, and who will pick you from the airport. It's closer, so you now think about it more definitively. Psychologists refer to this as construal-level theory.

Now, take those same dreams and aspirations and zoom in on their various aspects and begin working on them. As long as it remains abstract and as a big picture, then it can be done tomorrow because there is plenty of time to get this done. Bring that big picture closer to you so that you can see the small details necessary for completion. Focusing on concrete pieces of the big picture makes it more real and attainable. When we think of things concretely, we are more inclined to do them today. The practicality of this approach can be applied in numerous ways. It doesn't always have to pertain to big dreams and future goals. You can apply it to the simplest things. For example, your goal is to clean your house today. The kitchen is a disaster. The dirty-clothes hamper is overflowing. The carpet looks dusty, and it's crying for a good vacuuming, and the rest of the house is decorated with random pieces of mail, some opened and some unopened. Maybe this is just my home occasionally . . . or maybe you're just pretending this isn't your house too! Cleaning the entire house is abstract, and seeing it that way could make it an intimidating task to accomplish in 24 hours. Approach it more concretely: Today, I will get the laundry done and sort through the mail.

Tomorrow, I will organize the baby's room, sweep the floor, and run the vacuum. Behold, what seemed an impossible task is now completed, as you finished it in reasonable and attainable increments.

Lastly, ask yourself a series of "what if" questions to help you refocus and realign with your initiatives. Our "What if" questions tend to be focused on potential negative outcomes. For that reason, I want you to couple each negative "What if" question with a positive one. Transform your thinking.

What if it doesn't work out? Well, what if it works out better than expected?

What if I don't lose enough weight? What if you lose more weight than you originally planned?

What if the business doesn't make a lot of money? What if the business makes enough money where you can stop working full time and focus exclusively on your business?

What if they don't like my product? What if my product appeals to millions and sets trends one day?

What if they don't enjoy my music? What if my music presents a revolutionary sound and creativity to the music industry and changes the world?

What if they don't like my book? What if the pages I write become an annual best seller?

What if I can't? What if I hush and do?

I'm not here to guarantee odds. Success and failure are unavoidable facets of life. Yes, tomorrow is not promised; however, I'm sure most of you will be alive for a few more hours and probably even tomorrow to finish reading. There will be ups and downs. I'm not selling you any wolf tickets here. You will have to delay gratification to get to where you want. Maybe things will work out and maybe they won't. If they don't work out, maybe you need to re-strategize and try again. You have procrastinated long enough, and now it's time to take the next step of being real with yourself, identify what's really going on with you, and take charge of your attention, your focus, and yourself. The time for excuse-making has come to an end. We now lay procrastination to rest.

Ashes to ashes. Dust to dust. Make it happen!

Chapter 9

Make It Happen

"Jay, when you are focused and locked in on something, absolutely nothing stops you.

It's almost scary. When you are determined to do something, you find a way to make it happen."

—*Christine Hairston*

These highly motivational, encouraging, and empowering words came from my lovely wife, Christine. She may never understand just how deeply they touched me. I've been trying to impress and woo her ever since we met. As a matter of fact, she's the only woman I've ever really tried to impress. I never fully realized that about myself until she identified it and articulated it. "Make it happen" is the cornerstone of my work ethic. It does not matter if I'm faced with a tremendous task or more bills than I have money in a particular month. I always say to myself, "Make it happen." I want you to take on that same mindset. Regardless of any opposition to what you're pursuing and no matter how long it may take, *make it happen*.

People ask me all the time if *HushAndDo* is motivational speaking. My answer is always yes, but a yes answer alone is limiting. So often motivation here in the United States is geared toward our Western cultural value orientation of "doing." The work of *HushAndDo* is largely being—self-reflection, self-assessment, and transformational thinking, which leads to transformational living. To this point, we have explored many themes involving your heart and soul—the inward journey:

• We've silenced the many voices that compete to hold your attention. They ultimately form to overwhelm your thinking and decision-making. The silence goes for your own voice of doubt as well.

• Those who publicly declare their intentions are actually less likely to follow through in completing them. Competing voices and information overload cannot keep you from moving forward. You have permission to go.

• What do you truly desire more: your success or something else? What lies do you continue to believe about yourself as a result of deep wounding? Consider how it may affect your life situation and behavior.

• Fear can greatly affect your life situation as well. Remember, the *only way past it is through.* It's one thing to avoid fear, but if you're going to overcome it, then you must be willing to do something different. You have to change.

• Change is a necessary component for greatness. You're welcome to keep trying things the way you always have, but if you do, you're also welcoming slow death as well.

• You are much, and the world is waiting for you to manifest and come alive. Don't underestimate your significance to the global society. Expect victory and success wherever you are because your family, your co-workers, your church, and your community have one of the most valuable teammates in you. You are the greatest you of all time.

• The 50/50 Rule: 50 percent of the time, mind your own business. The other 50 percent of the time, stay out of other people's business. Mind your business and your own lane, please.

• Death to procrastination! You've put things off long enough. Your gift, time, and talent are too valuable to delay any longer. You have wonderful things to create, assist with, and contribute to the world, and it costs too much to procrastinate. Feeling motivated yet? Finally, I will present a bit of motivational discourse to encourage you to finish and make it happen in your life.

9.1 Rehearsing Victory

One of my seminary professors enjoyed rock-climbing, and he shared with me his strategy to help his students master the wall. Normal logic would assume that to climb the rock wall, you must start at the bottom and simply climb your way up until you get to the top and over the wall. My professor changed this approach. If it was a 100-foot wall, he would have his students begin their climb at 75 feet instead of from the floor. In a relatively fast time, the student would clear the wall. After a few repetitions of conquering a 25-foot climb, he would then begin them halfway up the wall, at 50 feet. The students would make the climb and clear the wall again. Soon after, the climb would start at 25 feet, leaving them a 75-foot climb. Are you catching the pattern? Finally, each student would start their climb from the ground level and climb 100 percent of the wall on their own with no assistance. Clearing the wall wasn't a new thing now, only the distance was. In this manner, they rehearsed success over and over. They achieved their 100-foot task with small victories and small steps. Clearing the wall multiple times was a sign of victory. Those victories, rehearsed over and over, built the confidence to take one more challenging task. They practiced winning instead of defeat. Success became a habit. I'm sure some students looked at that wall and predetermined that they could never scale its entirety. All it took was a little resolve, and what once seemed empty and impossible now became possible. They had a teacher who was willing to help them locate their strength deep within and draw it out. He reached in and pulled greatness out of them.

9.2 You and Peter: Something from Nothing

Peter was one of the first disciples to follow Jesus as His his ministry began. The crowds were pressing around Jesus to hear Him preach the Word of God by the Sea of Galilee. Jesus saw two empty boats by the sea's edge and chose to get into Peter's boat. It was left empty because they were washing their nets, presumably done fishing for the day. He requested that he put out a little farther from the land so He could sit down and teach the crowds. After He finished teaching, He told Peter, "Put out into the deep water and let down your nets for a catch." Though he initially objected because they had been fishing all night, Peter eventually complied and did as he was instructed. When they let down their nets, they caught so many fish that the nets began to break. There were so many fish that they signaled to the other boat to help them. Both vessels were filled to the point that they began to sink. Humbly astonished, Peter fell at Jesus' feet and implored Him to go away because he was a sinful man. He was absolutely amazed by the miraculous catch of fish and could barely move. His partners in fishing were there to witness the entire phenomenon, James and John. Jesus charged Peter saying, "Do not fear, from now on you will be catching men." When they had brought their boats to land, they left everything and followed Jesus, Luke 5:1–11 (NASB).

Something about the Sea of Galilee was special for Jesus and Peter. There they seem to have transformative experiences together. Do you recall Peter's adventurous advance over the stormy waters of a Galilean sea (Chapter 3)? Although *HushAndDo* is primarily an inward work, there remains an aspect of doing that cannot be ignored. May I suggest that it's important to have a designated place where you *HushAndDo*? Whether it be a space in your house, a special seat in a coffee shop, a certain trail in the Metroparks, or even in the confines of a boat, make sure you have a defined location earmarked for the work of your heart and the work of your hands. It should be a place you can go to for clarity, creativity, self-assessment, and stillness, where you cannot only meet yourself but meet with the Divine as well.

Peter and his crew had been fishing all night long and had caught nothing. They had apparently given up, as evidenced by their empty boats.

During that time, when fishermen washed their nets, it usually signified the end of a day's or night's work. Furthermore, washing nets was important because as they cast them into the water, they would grab anything within reach, including potentially dead fish, rocks, seaweed, and other debris. Jesus was not a fisherman. He was the son of a carpenter, so His lane was carpentry. Peter and his partners were fishermen by trade, so certainly they would understand fishing better than the carpenter would, right? They fished all night, to no avail. It seemed there were no fish. They toiled all night against the weather conditions, laboring in anticipation of a decent catch, tired and presumably disappointed, and still no fish. The wood artisan instructs them to try it again and to put out to deep water and let the nets down. Why would these expert fishermen be so inclined to listen to the suggestion of a woodworker? They had packed up their tools and were ready to head home, but Jesus was asking them to try it again but to go a little deeper this time. Peter followed His instructions and, fortunately for him, it resulted in more fish than they could imagine.

I creatively place myself in the shoes of Peter, subdued, as I marvel at such a great catch of fish, virtually unable to articulate myself, feeling rather lowercase in the presence of this miracle man. What would I have said? How would I have responded? Permit me some artistic license as I consider what could have been Peter's thought process that led him to leave everything and follow Jesus. I fancy Peter's reasoning went something like this:

"I've been working all night long trying to get something from nothing. There's no fish in here, yet we tried and tried the entire night. He comes along and suddenly He's able to pull fish from what I thought was an empty sea. I only saw nothingness, but somehow, He saw something; He saw fish. I'm just a fisherman, but maybe He sees something deeper in me. If He can pull many fish from a sea of nothing, then maybe He can pull purpose from me. Maybe He can pull much from the depths of my soul. I'll follow this man so I too can see in me what He sees in me."

9.3 Into Your Depths

Perhaps you, like Peter, have been working all night long, striving to accomplish things in your life. You've been working your whole life, toiling to discover who you are, what your purpose is, and what your contribution to the world will be. It's quite possible that currently you don't see much in yourself or think anything valuable is located in the depths of your being. Just like Peter and his co-workers, in some regard, you have already begun to wash your nets as well. You have already resigned yourself to the fact that wherever you are right now in life, this is your lot and all that it can be. *This is it.* You have closed up shop to the possibility of being and becoming more, accepting what seems to be a marginal existence right now. I may not understand fully what it's like to walk in your shoes or to work in your field or to have the responsibilities you do. However, I'm here to gently suggest that you go out a little deeper and cast your nets in profound waters. Cast them into the depths of your heart and soul and don't be afraid of whatever may come up. Yes, I'm hoping that it's a miraculous catch for you and a wonderful turn of events, but I realize your nets will also have some things in there that shouldn't be. Don't be afraid of that. Bring it all on board so you can sort through fish and debris—the things about you that are great and the things that beckon change. It doesn't matter what you see right now because the

Master sees great things in your depths. He Himself stowed them there and is waiting for you to dive into the deep to discover them. He's ready to pull some incredible things from your life. You simply must dare to deep dive. This is your charge to *DO*. Don't give up yet. Don't pack up and close down quite yet. I need you to try it again and make it happen, even if you're ready to quit. ***It's always too soon to give up when God is in it.***

The deep summons you. . . . Now, *hush* and *do*.

ENDNOTES

[1] All social media stats in this chapter come from http://www.statista.com (accessed December 12, 2017).

[2] Gordon Donnelly, "75 Super-Useful Facebook Statistics for 2018," *The Wordstream Blog,* accessed August 28, 2018, https://www.wordstream.com/blog/ws/2017/11/07/facebook-statistics.

[3] Salman Aslam, "Twitter by the Numbers: Stats, Demographics & Fun Facts," Omnicore, accessed August 28,2018, https://www.omnicoreagency.com/twitter-statistics/

[4] "Media Usage in an Internet Minute as of June 2018," Statista, accessed August 28, 2018. https://www.statista.com/statistics/195140/new-user-generated-content-uploaded- by-users-per-minute/.

[5] Musiq Soulchild, Feel the Real, "Shudawudacuda," SoulStar Music Company (SSMC), 2017, M4A.

[6] Ronald E. Brown, Live: Having Good Old Fashioned Church Part One. "There's a Storm Out on the Ocean," S.U.M. Music Group-1996, 331/3 rpm, LP.

[7] Peter M. Gollwitzer, Paschal Sheeran, Verena Michalski, and Andrea E. Seifert, "When Intentions Go Public: Does Social Reality Widen the Intention-Behavior Gap?" *Psychological Science* 20, no. 5 (Association for Psychological Science 2009): 612.

[8] Gollwitzer et al. 613.

[9] Gollwitzer et al. 616.

[10] Terry Wardle, Outrageous Love, Transforming Power: How the Holy Spirit Shapes You into the Likeness of Christ (Texas: Leafwood Publishers, 2004), 92.

[11] Terry Wardle, Healing Care, Healing Prayer: Helping the Broken Find Wholeness in Christ (Texas: Leafwood Publishers, 2001), 140.

[12] "Peter Don't Be Afraid," Soul Searchers, *Divine Sounds: Best of Classic Gospel,* Peacock Gospel Classics, 1998.

[13] Susan Jeffers, *Feel the Fear and Do It Anyway* (New York: The Ballantine Publishing Group, 2007), 13–16.

[14] Jeffers, Feel the Fear and Do It Anyway, 15.

[15] Felicity A. Cowdrey and Linda Walz, "Exposure Therapy for Fear of Spiders in an Adult with Learning Disabilities: A Case Report," *British Journal of Learning Disabilities* 43 (John Wiley & Sons Ltd., 2014): 76.

[16] Noam Shpancer, "Overcoming Fear: The Only Way Out is Through," *Psychology Today*

(September 2010), https://www.psychologytoday.com/us/blog/insight-therapy/201009/overcoming-fear-the-only-way-out-is-through (accessed July 5, 2018).

[17] Robert E Quinn, *Deep Change: Discovering the Leader Within* (California: Jossey-Bass, 1996).

[18] Quinn, 18.

[19] Quinn, 66.

[20] Quinn, 11.

[21] Charlet Lewis, I Had to Change: Conquering My Past To Embrace My Future (Virginia: TL65, 2017).

[22] Robert E Quinn, *Deep Change: Discovering the Leader Within* (California: Jossey-Bass), 20.

[23] Quinn, *Deep Change*, 52.

[24] Stevie Wonder, "Higher Ground," *Innervisions*, Motown Records, 1973.

[25] Wonder, "Higher Ground," 1973.

[26] Howard Thurman as **quoted in** *Violence Unveiled* by Gil Bailie (The Crossroads Publishing Company, November 1996).

[27] James Herbert, "Cavaliers Forward LeBron James Called Himself the Best Player In the World after the Game." **Quoted by** LeBron James (CBS Sports Digital: June 2015).

[28] The Oxford Dictionary of Quotations, 3rd ed., s.v."Island."

[29] Plato, *Plato Republic*, Translated by G. M. A. Grube, Revised by C. D. C. Reeve (Indianapolis/Cambridge: Hackett Publishing Company, Inc., 1992).

[30] Fainos Mangena, "African Ethics through Ubuntu: A Postmodern Exposition," *Africology: The Journal of Pan African Studies* 9, no. 2 (April 2016): 67.

[31] David W. Lutz, "African 'Ubuntu' Philosophy and Global Management," *Journal of Business Ethics* 84, sup. 3 (Springer 2009): 314.

[32] J. S. Mbiti, *African Religions & Philosophy*, 2nd ed. (Nairobi: East African Educational Publishers, 1969), 215.

[33] Manal Ghosain, "The Art and Science of Minding Your Own Business," *One With Now* (June 2012), http://www.onewithnow.com/minding-your-own-business/ (accessed December 28, 2017).

[34] Judith B. White, Ellen J. Langer, Leeat Yariv, and John C. Welch IV, "Frequent Social Comparisons and Destructive Emotions and Behaviors: The Dark Side of Social Comparisons," *Journal of Adult Development* 13, no. 1 (Springer Science + Business Media, Inc. March 2006): 36.

[35] White et al. "Frequent Social Comparisons and Destructive Emotions and Behaviors," 37.

[36] Justine Curwen, "Social Comparison: An Unavoidable Upward or Downward Spiral," *Positive Psychology Articles* (April 2016), http://www.positivepsychologicalprogram.com/social-comparison/ (accessed February 15, 2018).

[37] Sonja Lyubomirsky and Lee Ross, "Hedonic Consequences of Social Comparison: A Contrast of

Happy and Unhappy People," *Journal of Personality and Social Psychology* 73, no. 6: (January 1998): 1141-57.

38 Judith B. White, Ellen J. Langer, Leeat Yariv, and John C. Welch IV, "Frequent Social Comparisons and Destructive Emotions and Behaviors: The Dark Side of Social Comparisons," *Journal of Adult Development* 13, no. 1 (March 2006), https://doi.org/ 10.1007/s10804-006-9005-0.

39 Justine Curwen, "Social Comparison: An Unavoidable Upward or Downward Spiral," *Positive Psychology Articles* (April 2016), http://www.positivepsychologicalprogram.com/social-comparison/ (accessed February 15, 2018).

40 Curwen, "Social Comparison," 2016.

41 Curwen, 2016.

42 C. Carmona, B.P. Buuna, J.M. Peiro, I. Rodrigues, and M. J. Bravo, "Do Social Comparison and Coping Styles Play a Role in the Development of Burnout? Cross-sectional and Longitudinal findings," *Journal of Occupational and Organisational Psychology* (2006): 79, 85-99,

quoted in Justine Curwen, "Social Comparison: An Unavoidable Upward or Downward Spiral," *Positive Psychology Articles* (April 2016).

43 The Winans, "Tomorrow," *Tomorrow*, Intersound Records, 1984.

44 John Lea, *The Boy's Own Paper* 37, Iss. 3 (United Kingdom: January 1915).

45 Joseph R. Ferrari, *Still Procrastinating: The No Regrets Guide to Getting It Done* (New Jersey: John Wiley & Sons Inc, 2010), 13.

46 Ferrari, Still Procrastinating, 13.

47 Ferrari, Still Procrastinating, 47.

48 Timothy A. Pychyl, Richard W. Morin, and Brian R. Salmon, "Procrastination and the Planning Fallacy: An Examination of the Study Habits of University Students," special issue, *Journal of Social Behavior and Personality* 15 (Select Press 2000): 135-150.

49 Educational Development Centre, Carleton University, "Teaching Talk: Helping Students Who Procrastinate (Tim Pychyl)," YouTube Video, 58:43,

Dec. 17, 2012, https://www.youtube.com/watch?v=mhFQA998WiA&t=566s.

50 Ferrari, Still Procrastinating? The no-regrets guide to getting it done, 121.

51 Roy F. Baumeister and Todd F. Heatherton, "Self-Regulation Failure: An Overview," *Psychological Inquiry* 7 (Lawrence Erlbaum 1996): 2.

52 Baumeister and Heatherton, "Self-Regulation Failure," 3.

53 Joseph R. Ferrari, Still Procrastinating? The No-Regrets Guide to Getting It Done (New Jersey: John Wiley & Sons, Inc., 2010),96

54 Ferrari, Still Procrastinating? The No-Regrets Guide to Getting It Done, 96.

BIBLIOGRAPHY

Aslam, Salman. "Facebook by the Numbers: Stats, Demographics & Fun Facts." *Omnicore*. Omnicore Agency. Accessed August 28, 2018. https://www.omnicoreagency.com/facebook-statistics/

Baumeister, Roy F., Dianne Tice and Kathleen Vohs. "The Strength Model of Self-Regulation: Conclusions from the Second Decade of Willpower Research." *Perspectives on Psychological Science*, 13

(March 2018): 141–145. https://doi.org/10.1177/1745691617716946

Baumeister, Roy F., and Todd F. Heatherton. "Self-Regulation Failure: An Overview." Psychological Inquiry 7 (1996): 1–15.

Cowdrey, Felicity A., and Linda Walz. "Exposure Therapy for Fear of Spiders in an Adult with Learning Disabilities: a Case Report." *British Journal of Learning Disabilities* 43 (John Wiley & Sons, Ltd., 2014): 75–82.

Curwen, Justine. "Social Comparison: An Unavoidable Upward or Downward Spiral." *Positive Psychology Program*, (April 2016). Accessed February 15, 2018. http://www.positivepsychologicalprogram.com/social-comparison/

Educational Development Centre, Carleton University. "Teaching Talk: Helping Students Who Procrastinate (Tim Pychyl)." YouTube Video, 58:43. Dec. 17, 2012. https://www.youtube.com/watch?v=mhFQA998WiA&t=566s.

"Facebook. Number of Daily Active Facebook Users Worldwide as of 2nd Quarter 2018 (in millions)." Accessed August 28, 2018. https://www.statista.com/statistics/346167 /facebook-global-dau/.

"Facebook. Number of Facebook users in the United States from 2015 to 2022 (in millions)." Accessed August 28, 2018. https://www.statista.com/statistics/408971 / number-of-us-facebook-users/.

Ferrari, Joseph R. Still Procrastinating? The No-Regrets Guide to Getting It Done. New Jersey: John Wiley & Sons Inc., 2010.

Foster, Richard J. Celebration of Discipline: The Path to Spiritual Growth. SanFrancisco:Harper, 1998.

Ghosain, Manal. "The Art and Science of Minding Your Own Business." *One With Now* (June 2012). http://www.onewithnow.com/ minding-your-own-business/.

Shpancer, Noam. "Overcoming Fear: The Only Way Out is Through." *Psychology Today*, (September 2010). https://www.psychologytoday. com/us/blog/insight-therapy/201009/overcoming-fear-the-onlyway- out-is-through.

Gollwitzer, Peter M., Paschal Sheeran, Verena Michalski, and Andrea E. Seifert. "When Intentions Go Public: Does Social Reality Widen the Intention-Behavior Gap?" *Psychological Science* 20, no. 5 (Association for Psychological Science, 2009): 612–618.

Jeffers, Susan. *Feel the Fear and Do It Anyway*. New York: The Ballantine Publishing Group, 1987.

Lewis, Charlet. I Had to Change: Conquering My Past to Embrace My Future. Virginia: TL65, 2017.

Lutz, David W. "African 'Ubuntu' Philosophy and Global Management." *Journal of Business Ethics* 84, sup. 3 (Springer 2009): 313–328.

Mangena, Fainos. "African Ethics through Ubuntu: A Postmodern Exposition." *Africology: The Journal of Pan African Studies* 9, no. 2 (Itibari M. Zulu April 2016): 66–80.

Mbiti, J. S. *African Religions & Philosophy*. 2nd ed. Nairobi: East African Educational Publishers, 1969.

McCrea, Sean M., Nira Liberman, Yaacov Trope, and Steven J. Sherman. "Construal Level and Procrastination." *Psychological Science* 19, no. 12 (Association for Psychological Science 2008): 1308–1314.

McMickle, Marvin. *An Encyclopedia of African American Christian Heritage*. Valley Forge, Pennsylvania: Judson Press, 2002.

McNeal, Reggie. A Work of Heart. Understanding How God Shapes Spiritual Leaders. San Francisco: Jossey-Bass, 2000.

Mischel, Walter. The Marshmallow Test: Why Self-Control Is the Engine of Success. New York: Little Brown and Company, 2014.

Muhammad, Elijah. *Message to the Blackman*. Phoenix, Arizona: Secretarius MEMPS Publications, 1973.

Owens, Gregory, Christine G. Bowman, and Charles A. Dill. "Overcoming Procrastination: The Effect of Implementation Intentions." *Journal of Applied Social Psychology* 38, no. 2

(Winter 2008): 366–384. https://doi.org/10.1111/j.1559-1816.2007.00309.x

Plato. *Plato Republic*. Translated by G. M. A. Grube. Revised by C. D. C. Reeve. Indianapolis/Cambridge: Hackett Publishing Company, Inc., 1992.

Pychyl, Timothy A., Richard W. Morin, and Brian R. Salmon. "Procrastination and the Planning Fallacy: An Examination of the Study Habits of University Students." Special Issue, *Journal of Social Behavior and Personality* 15 (Select Press 2000): 135–150.

Quinn, Robert E. *Deep Change: Discovering the Leader Within*. California: Jossey-Bass, 1996.

Radzik, Linda. "On Minding Your Own Business: Differentiating Accountability Relations within the Moral Community." *Social Theory & Practice* 37, no. 4 (October 2011): 574–598.

Rath, Tom, and Barry Conchie. Strengths Based Leadership: Great Leaders, Teams, and Why People Follow. New York: Gallup Press, 2008.

Sirois, Fuschia M. "Procrastination and Counterfactual Thinking: Avoiding What Might Have Been." British Journal of Social Psychology 43 (December 2010): 269–286.

Soulchild, Musiq. "Shudawudacuda." *Feel the Real.* Soul Star Music Company (SSMC) Management. M4A. 2017.

Stohr, Karen. "Minding Others' Business." *Pacific Philosophical Quarterly* 90 (University of Southern California and Blackwell Publishing Ltd. 2009): 116–139. https://doi.org/ 10.1111/j.1468-0114.2009.01331.x

Tal-Or, Nurit. "Bragging in the Right Context: Impressions Formed of Self-Promoters Who Create a Context for Their Boasts." *Social Influence* 5 (2010): 23–39. http://dx.doi.org/10.1080/15534510903160480

The Oxford Dictionary of Quotations, 3rd ed., s.v. "Island."

The Winans. "Tomorrow." *Tomorrow.* Intersound Records, 1984.

Wardle, Terry. Healing Care Healing Prayer: Helping the Broken Find Wholeness in Christ. Texas: Leafwood Publishers, 2001.

Wardle, Terry. Outrageous Love Transforming Power: How the Holy Spirit Shapes You into the Likeness of Christ. Texas: Leafwood Publishers, 2004.

Wheeler, Marcus. "Self-Sufficiency and the Greek City." *Journal of the History of Ideas* 16, no. 3 (June 1955): 416–420.

White, Judith B., Ellen J. Langer, Leeat Yariv, and John C. Welch IV. "Frequent Social Comparisons and Destructive Emotions and Behaviors: The Dark Side of Social Comparisons." *Journal of Adult Development* 13, no. 1 (March 2006): 36–44.

Wonder, Stevie. "Higher Ground." *Innervisions.* Motown Records, 1973.